Whimsical Teddy Bears
15 Patterns &
Design Techniques

Creative Crafters

Whimsical Teddy Bears
15 Patterns &
Design Techniques
by Neysa A. Phillippi

Portfolio Press

Dedications

This book would not have been possible without editor Krystyna Poray Goddu of Portfolio Press. We first spoke when she was writing an article about artist Karen Meer of *"The Mad Hatted Bear"* for *Teddy Bear Review* magazine. We had quite an interesting conversation about teddy bears and the "Artists for Artists" tours I present to Europe for Teddy Bear artists and collectors.

And without the following I wouldn't be here...

Fatso, Sad Sack, Chicken George, Quasimoto, Charley, Gino and countless other misfits for my inspiration.
To my mom and dad whose understanding of how important freedom and imagination were to a child's spirit.
Allowing me to be myself and let my imagination run as wild as it and I did as a child.
To my husband Gerry McKinney for his continuing support of my individuality.

Most people will tell you that if in your entire lifetime you can count on one hand five true, always-standing-beside-you and loving friends, that you are truly blessed. I must have six fingers on one hand because Terry Hayes, Sharon Dressman, Celia Baham, Linda Munnell, Trudy Jacobson and Robert Zacher are mine, to them I dedicate this book.

Acknowledgements

I would like to thank everyone who helped with spelling when my computer had no idea what I was talking about; my proofreaders Celia, Trudy and Sue Krieg; and the artists for their invaluable tips and hints that I hope have made this book informative and the patterns fun.

All patterns are for personal use only, and are not to be mass-produced for resale in any size including published reductions or enlargements.

First edition/First printing

To purchase additional copies of this book, please contact:
Portfolio Press, 130 Wineow Street, Cumberland, MD 21502
877-737-1200

Library of Congress Catalog Card Number 00-135262
ISBN 0-942620-48-8

Project Editor: Krystyna Poray Goddu
Design and Production: Tammy S. Blank

Cover photo, interior photography and drawings by Neysa A. Phillippi
Cover design by John Vanden-Heuvel Design

Printed and bound in Korea

Contents

Introduction 6

Design Basics... and Beyond 8
Side Head 10
Head Gussets 13
Ears...17
Bodies...18
Arms...21
Legs 24
Paw Pads 25
Foot Pads 26
Tails 27
Noses 28
Jointing 29
Stitches 30
Open Mouth...............................31
Double-Jointed Head 32

Basic Directions
Cutting out the pattern.....................33
Laying out your pattern pieces 33
Pinning..34
Tips/Thread 34
Side Head – Head Gusset 35
Ears 35
Body 36
Arms 36
Legs 37
Leg to Foot Pads.............................37

Finishing
Types of eyes 38
Stuffing the head........................39
Attaching the head joint 39
Eye placement 39
Noses 39
Ears 40
Directions for jointing 41
Stuffing the arms/legs/body.............43

Patterns
Beasley 44
Bubbles.......................................50
Buckshot.....................................56
Bumble 62
Cal 68
Dusty 74
Grizz..80
Kim Moon 88
Klondike.......................................94
Molly 100
Sidney 106
Taylor 112
Vladimir.......................................118
Wilbur..126
Winston 132

Artists' Secrets for Making Better Bears 142
Invaluable Sources 144

Introduction

Artists are type A personalities. There is never a dull moment, never an idle hand, the brain is always functioning, always right, and there are no games when it comes to designing and money. There is always a note pad and pen on the nightstand and in the bathroom, and we stop in the middle of a sentence when an idea hits.

Personal life—what's that? We have no time to socialize, with the exception of teddy bear shows, as creating has taken over our lives. The drive to create is sometimes stronger than sex, marriage, laundry, food—but never chocolate. For some, the act of creation is their only friend.

My life as a teddy bear artist began a few years after I graduated from the Art Institute of Pittsburgh with a degree in Photography/Multi-Media. I was freelancing as an agricultural photographer, delivering pizzas and working in the advertising department of Gimbels in Pittsburgh, PA as a Graphic Arts Technician. My best friend Adrienne Sempr kept taking me to a toy store across the street from Gimbels where she purchased dolls, I had no interest in dolls but a little bear from Gund caught my eye. I purchased my first teddy bear. I had grown up on a farm; who needed stuffed animals? All the misfits—those with medical problems or those orphaned or rejected by their mothers—ended up at the house. Thinking back, I realize those critters affected my outlook on life and my creative juices.

I made my first bear after my inspiration to buy a Steiff bear inspired my husband's comment: "how much did that cost?" I had always been an artist in some form, and wanted a loom so that I could expand my repertoire to include weaving. But I needed a way to make extra money to buy the loom of my dreams so I took that first teddy bear to work and came home with orders for twenty. The loom sat in a box for two years, as teddy bears became my passion. In 1984, I quit my job and moved to the country. I exhibited my cloth dolls, bears and weavings at art and craft shows. In 1985, I met Terry Hayes, who became my mentor. She encouraged me to try teddy bear shows. It took me until 1989 to find the courage to exhibit at my first bear show. That day weaving and dollmaking ended for me. Encouraged by other artists, collectors and sales I embarked on the adventure of my life.

My company, Purely Neysa, became a reality. Even then, though, I had no idea I would soon be attending as many as twenty shows a year, designing, selling patterns, teaching workshops, design classes and presenting tours to Europe, let alone writing this book!
At my first bear show in Ohio, I met several artists who, like me, were just starting out and established artists such as Linda Henry, Sharon Dressman and Jenny Krantz. Our promoter had a party for us the first night. The sharing of ideas, suppliers, tips and hints for creating better bears amazed me; in the craft world my experience had been that nothing is shared for fear of being copied.

Teddy bear people are the most caring and sharing people I have ever met. There is an unspoken rule that ideas shared will not be copied into a replica of their design. Ideas are "mulled" over and the thought process begins. Ninety-nine percent of the time the results look nothing like anyone else's work—which is how it should be. I can credit the information in this book to my own trial and error as well as to the expertise and advice of the many artists who have crossed my path in the past seventeen years.

My first bears were fairly traditional in design and made in plush when "only mohair makes a bear" was a common phrase. What I and my colleagues make are called "artist bears." If art comes in a variety of media, from sculptures made of junk welded together to marble statues, then teddy bears made of plush, mohair, wood or other materials are art. I have always believed this and I still do. I am pleased to see plush bears of quality abound. I'm a firm believer in being an individual, and in the phrase: "your time will come!"

I feel that my time came with my first trip to Europe. In my travels with my "Artists for Artists" European Tours over the past eight years, I and "we" as a group have tried to share with the European market and the world our friendship, our ideas, and our bears. What we have received back from all the artists and collectors we have befriended is much more precious than all the ideas in the world. Artist bears in Europe as well as in the rest of the world represent some of the most ingenious and creative work I have seen in years. I come home from each trip with the challenge and inspiration to design a better and more creative bear. Why not come along and experience for yourself the wonders of the world's teddy bears?

My introduction of **"Patterns of Bears Gone "Buy"** in the spring of 2000, featuring forty of my retired designs, evolved from a variety of factors. These included market changes, overwork and health concerns as well as my growing desires to expand my tour business, to write and to spend more time having a "normal" life with time for my husband. (My definition of normal is to work eight hours a day, five days a week instead of fourteen hours a day, seven days a week with no time off for good behavior.)

My hands are showing signs of carpal tunnel syndrome. Although designing and making creatures is my life, I thought: "why not patterns?" Let's face it: artists all have retired patterns sitting in boxes collecting dust. If you listen closely to those boxes, you may hear voices calling: "help, let me out of here, let someone love me!" That is, if you believe teddy bears talk and can live forever if you let them.

I hope the following basics of design will be a starting place for those of you who are making your first bear and perhaps a new way of thinking for those of you who are experienced artists. Enjoy the patterns and remember your imagination!

Design Basics... and Beyond
The Basic Bear and where to start?

Patterns and Kits: Everywhere you look, patterns and kits are available: at department stores, fabric stores, in craft and bear magazines, even from artists such as myself. You will find patterns for: jointed and unjointed bears, two-piece heads, three-piece heads, two-piece bodies, plastic joints, cotter pins, glass eyes, plastic safety eyes and so on. Purchase a sampling of these patterns, study the directions, the way they are drawn, the darts, bent or straight arms—you don't even have to make them all, though it does help. Buying not just bear patterns but patterns for other animals will give you more insight as to different design techniques. In my opinion, there is no wrong or right way to make a bear as long as your pattern pieces fit together.

Getting the feel for design, developing a style: Making creatures from different patterns and designs will not only give you the insight as to how it all works, but you will also, in time, develop a style. The artist learns from purchased patterns and from trial and error. The crafter continues to use purchased patterns, perhaps making a few changes and using them over and over again. In my opinion, an artist changes and grows constantly as the days and years go by.

Taking design classes and workshops: Taking classes will further your knowledge of design. Most artist believe that if you come out of a class with one good tip, it was worthwhile. Each artist has his or her own methods and techniques. A good teacher will share his or her knowledge and will do his or her best to answer all your questions. Some teddy bear artists have no art background at all; some are not sculptors; some (like me) couldn't copy a Steiff or any other bear no matter how hard they tried. Artists do not know everything. When teaching, we try to stimulate the students to think for themselves, and sometimes we the teachers learn from our students, or through our own teaching discover a new approach to a common problem or design technique.

What appeals to you: Through working with patterns, taking classes and reading magazines we discover what appeals to us personally. Through trying different pattern designs we find what works for us and what doesn't. This leads many to enter the world of original creations. Creative control is the final step to creating completely original designs.

What you do does not have to make sense to others as long as it works for you: Once you have absorbed all the information you can possibly handle, your bears begin to take on a life of their own. If you are making bears for self-gratification, what you create is always acceptable. If you plan to sell your creatures, however, and they are different from the norm, you have to understand, as I have, that a vast majority of collectors will think you're way out there. As to where "there" is—your guess is as good as my husband's. My father taught me to be a dreamer, a thinker and a doer; my mother taught me to be a seamstress. Each of us may do the same things differently. I stuff my head, attach the eyes, then the ears, and then the nose. Others may stuff the head; joint it, stuff the entire bear, then finish the face. If your method works for you, by all means do it! The same goes for choosing eyes, joints, yarns and fabrics.

Pattern design: Patterns can be designed in many different ways. I create by seeing something in my mind and then drawing it, but not everyone can do this. Some like to sketch from photographs of real bears or teddy bears. If you draw free hand you don't have to be a Rembrandt or even a Norman Rockwell to create a bear. Some of you may remember art classes in school where you were taught to draw circles for the torso and head, ovals for the arms and legs...or anatomy classes in biology. Some very talented artists start with an idea and make a three-dimensional prototype. However you get to the finished pattern is the right way for you.

Proportions can start with a balanced look—or by going off the deep end: One way to begin is to draw free hand, looking at yourself in a mirror or using a friend for a model, noting the contours of the body to design a human-like bear. If you want to create a realistic bear, find the best book available with real bears and lots of photographs. Sculpting a figure first, as mentioned previously, is another method. Using graph paper is a way to achieve a more proportioned and traditional design. If you're like me, heaven help you—you just do it.

Designing the pattern pieces: Designing is limited only by your imagination. The following design techniques will help you develop a style of your own. I've presented examples of heads, bodies, arms, legs, ears, and tails, based upon basic design techniques. I have also added a few optional or advanced ideas for you to contemplate. Bear in mind that these are only a few of the design techniques available.

Side Heads Looking up and down

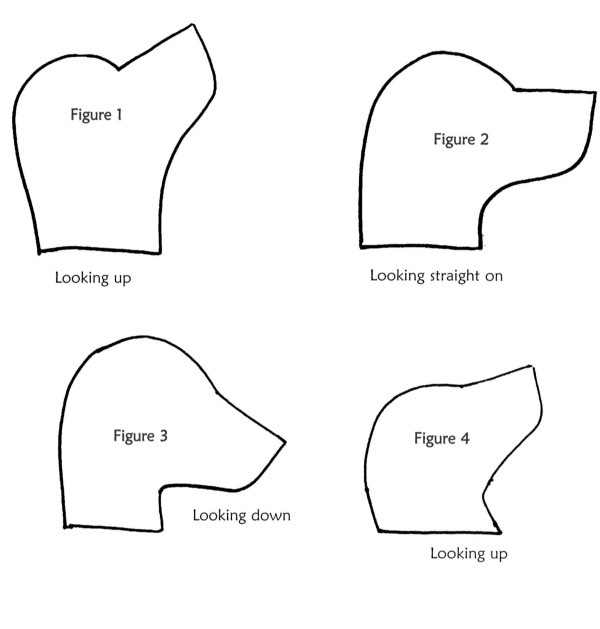

Figure 1

Looking up

Figure 2

Looking straight on

Figure 3

Looking down

Figure 4

Looking up

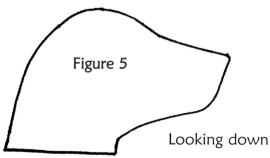

Figure 5

Looking down

Side Heads — darts

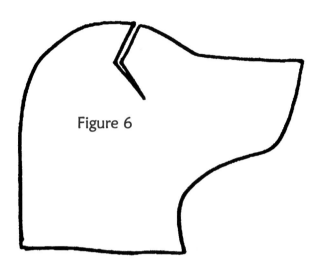

Figure 6

This dart places the ears at an angle when you sew the ears in to the dart. If you want the ears to be positioned straight with no curve, make the dart straight.

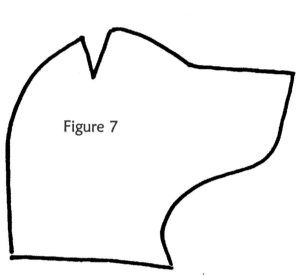

Figure 7

A dart placed on the top of the side head will give an extra curve to the top of the head.

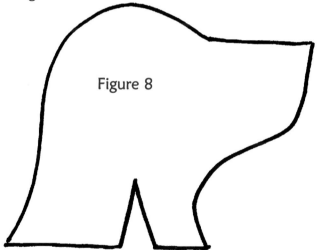

Figure 8

A neck dart makes a large neck opening smaller, which helps when drawing in the neck around the head joint. It will also create "cheeks."

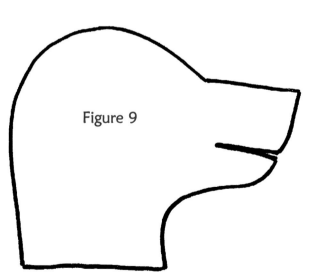

Figure 9

A mouth slit placed on the lower 1/3 of the muzzle is used to create an open-mouth bear (more about this later).

Optional Side Heads

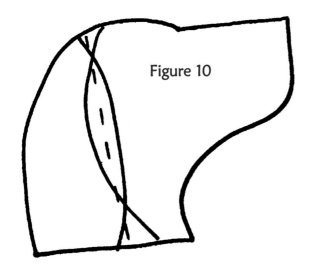

Figure 10

Figure 10 shows how to create a two-piece Side Head. Start by drawing a one-piece Side Head. Draw a line through the head at approximately the area the ear will be placed, as shown by the dotted line. Arc your shape as shown to create a rounded appearance. Trace each of the two pieces, then add the ears to both of them and you have a two-piece Side Head with the ears attached.

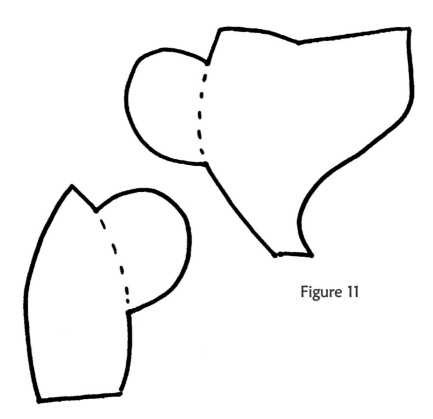

Figure 11

To use this optional side head with the ear included in the design: after sewing the two side head pieces together, top stitch the seam line (as shown with the dotted line in **Figure 11**). This creates a flat unstuffed ear. When stuffing the head the ear will cup forward. Don't forget to add ¼-inch seam allowances.

Head Gussets all shapes and sizes

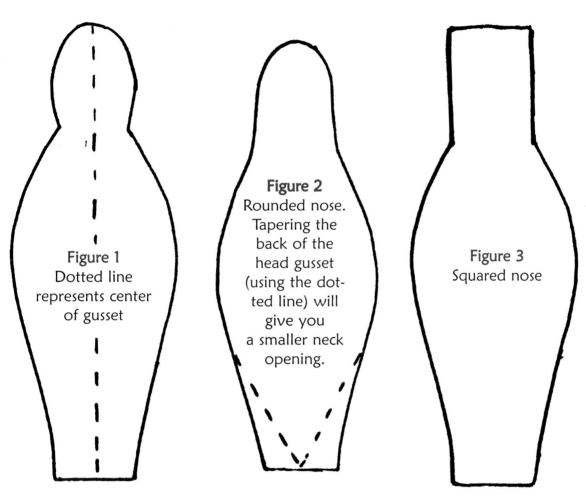

Figure 1
Dotted line
represents center
of gusset

Figure 2
Rounded nose.
Tapering the
back of the
head gusset
(using the dot-
ted line) will
give you
a smaller neck
opening.

Figure 3
Squared nose

Here are some optional designs for creating different head shapes and appearances. In **Figure 1** the dotted line represents the center of the gusset. **Figure 2** shows an optional design with the dotted line.

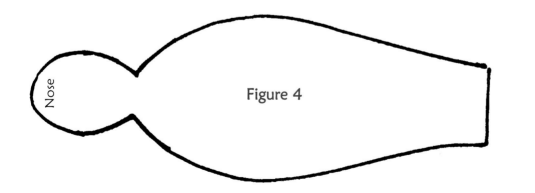

Nose

Figure 4

This gusset will
bring the eyes
closer together,
with no need
for needle
sculpture.

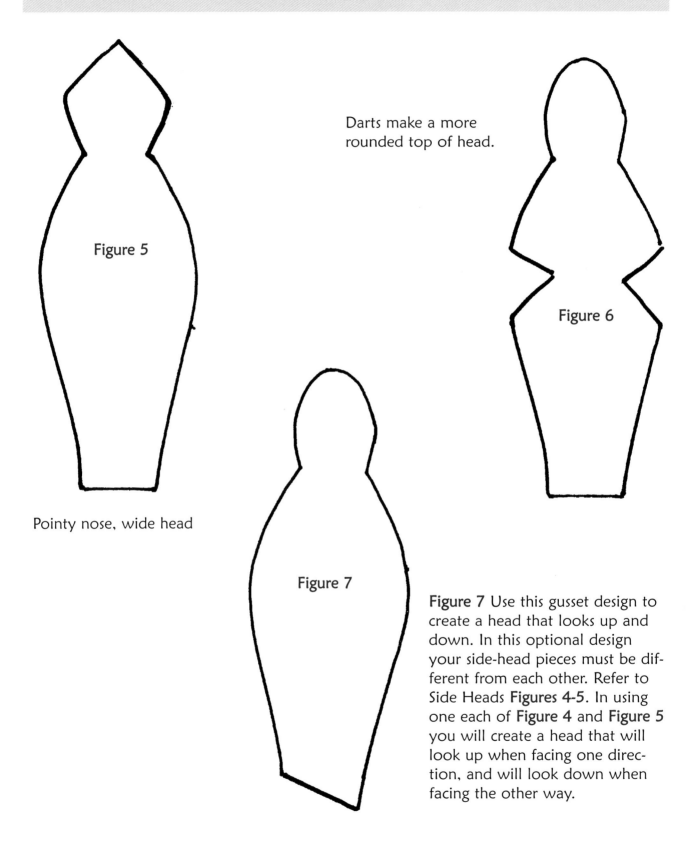

Figure 5

Pointy nose, wide head

Darts make a more rounded top of head.

Figure 6

Figure 7

Figure 7 Use this gusset design to create a head that looks up and down. In this optional design your side-head pieces must be different from each other. Refer to Side Heads **Figures 4-5.** In using one each of **Figure 4** and **Figure 5** you will create a head that will look up when facing one direction, and will look down when facing the other way.

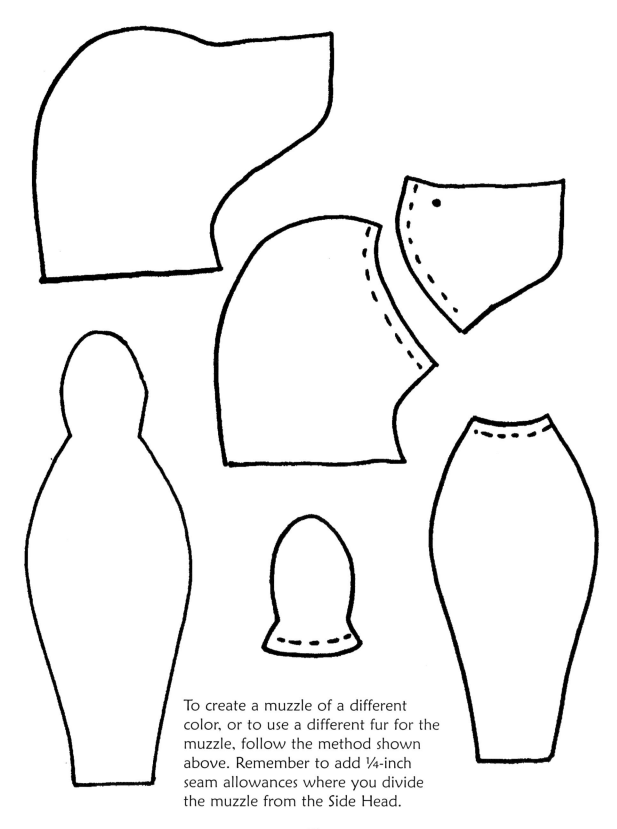

To create a muzzle of a different color, or to use a different fur for the muzzle, follow the method shown above. Remember to add ¼-inch seam allowances where you divide the muzzle from the Side Head.

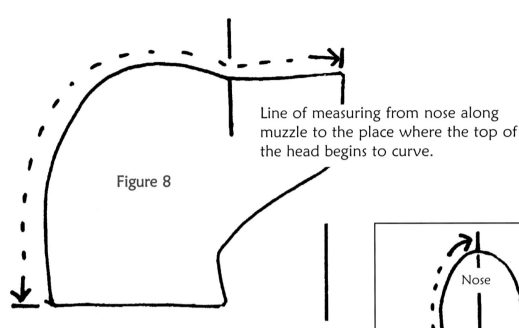

Figure 8

Line of measuring from nose along muzzle to the place where the top of the head begins to curve.

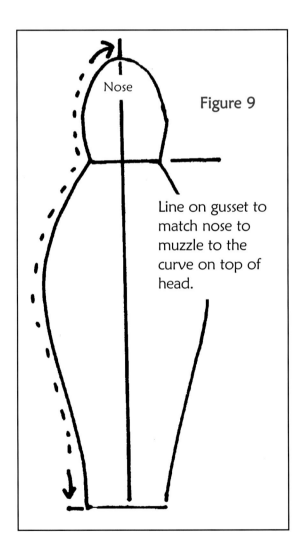

Nose

Figure 9

Line on gusset to match nose to muzzle to the curve on top of head.

Start with a blank piece of paper. Using a ruler, or any straight edge, draw a line down the center. Fold the paper along this line, set aside.

Working with the head shape you want to make, use a string to measure. Start at the tip of the nose, run it along the top of the side head and end at the base of the neck as shown by the dotted line in Figure 8. *Add at least 1/2 inch to your measurement to allow for fabric stiffness or stretch.

This length of string now represents the outside curve of your side head and your gusset length from the center front (center of nose) to the neck on one side as shown by the dotted line in Figure 9.

Next, measure from the tip of the nose on the side head to the place where your muzzle becomes the curve for the top of the head, as shown in Figure 8, by the solid line running horizontally through the muzzle or eye placement area. Measure using the string you have for the gusset. This measure represents the length—the area or measure for making the gusset narrow to meet the shape of the side head. Figure 9. What you have left in string length forms the top of the head from the horizontal line or the eye placement area to the neck.

Take the paper you folded earlier and place your string along the line. Using the string, form the shape of the head gusset. This folded paper represents half of the gusset, and allows you to cut the paper after you have determined your gusset shape. Cutting along the drawn line on the folded paper will give you the exact image on the other side, thus giving you a complete head gusset.

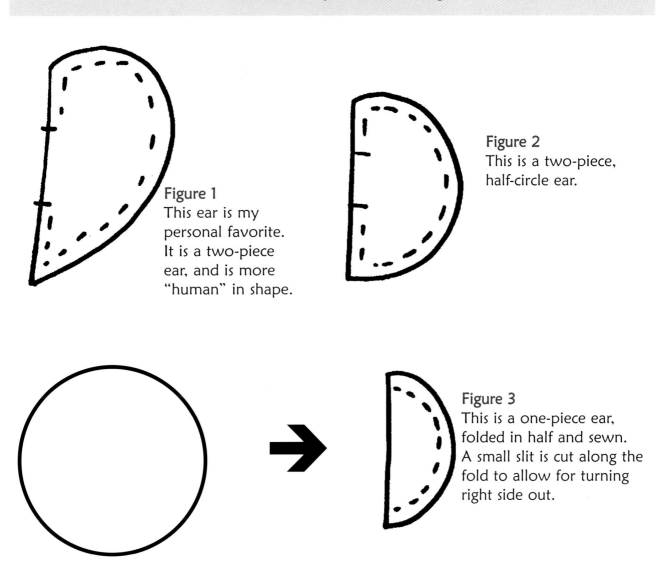

Figure 1
This ear is my personal favorite. It is a two-piece ear, and is more "human" in shape.

Figure 2
This is a two-piece, half-circle ear.

Figure 3
This is a one-piece ear, folded in half and sewn. A small slit is cut along the fold to allow for turning right side out.

Figure 4
This ear has a dart, which creates a curved ear. If you sew on this ear after the head is stuffed or sew it into the seam as shown in Side Head Darts **Figure 6 (page 11)** you will have a permanent curve and a more perfectly shaped ear.

All versions of the ears can be sewn into the head in **Figure 6**

Bodies two-piece

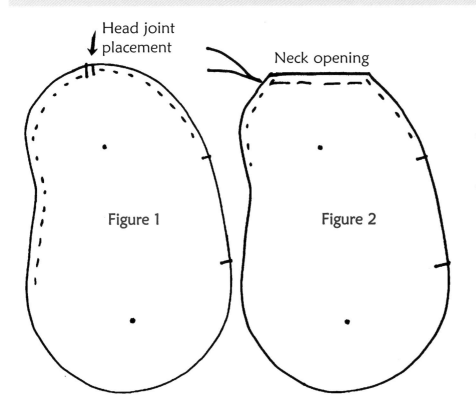

Head joint placement

Neck opening

Figure 1

Figure 2

Figure 1
Standard "normal" two-piece body

Figure 2
This body is open at the top to allow for the neck joint. Closing requires a gathering stitch (also called a running stitch or basting stitch) to draw in the opening, leaving only enough room for the head joint to pass through. This is a bulky way to joint and also creates a weak spot on the finished bear.

Bodies two-piece, darts, pot bellies

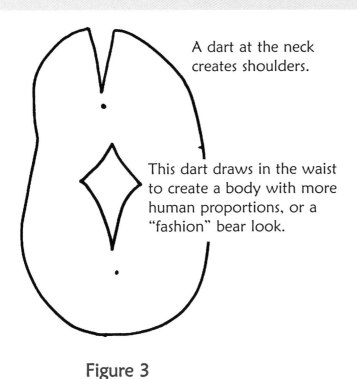

A dart at the neck creates shoulders.

This dart draws in the waist to create a body with more human proportions, or a "fashion" bear look.

A distended stomach creates that "pot-bellied" appearance.

Figure 3

Figure 4

Bodies two-piece, where to leave open for stuffing and jointing

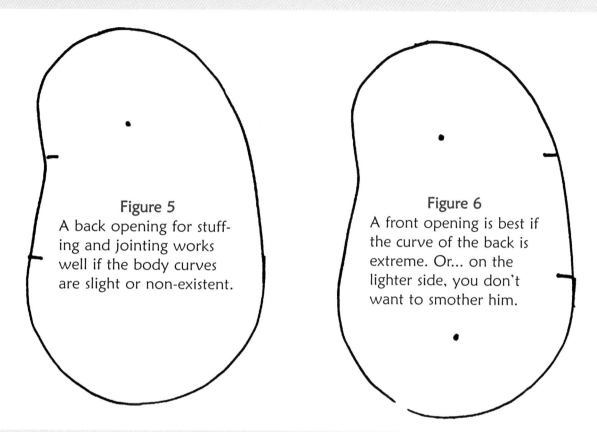

Figure 5
A back opening for stuffing and jointing works well if the body curves are slight or non-existent.

Figure 6
A front opening is best if the curve of the back is extreme. Or... on the lighter side, you don't want to smother him.

Bodies four-piece

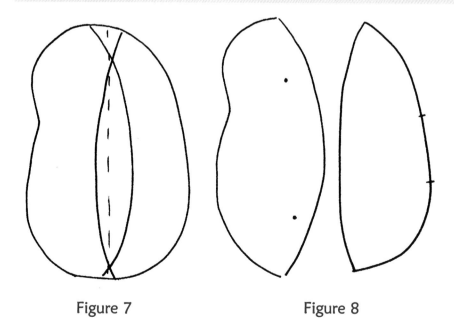

This four-piece body creates a fatter-looking bear. Start by drawing a two-piece body as shown in **Figure 7**. Draw a line through the body's center, as shown by the dotted line.
Arch your shape as shown to create a rounded appearance. Trace the two pieces you have now created, being sure to add ¼-inch seam allowance to the new arc shape you have created.

Figure 7   Figure 8

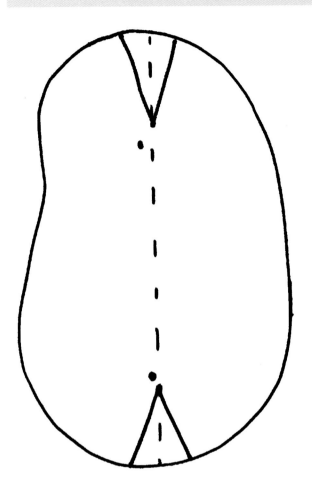

Figure 9
Body darts create extra shaping for shoulders and hips, and allow the arms and legs to fit tighter or closer to the body, creating a smoother look. If you have no darts, the limbs will stand out or protrude away from the body.

Figure 10
This separation of the body gives you the pieces to create a Panda. Changing the location of the split will accommodate the look of clothing as for **Vladimir (page 118)**. This method can also be used on the head, arms and legs. Don't forget to add your ¼-inch seam allowance.

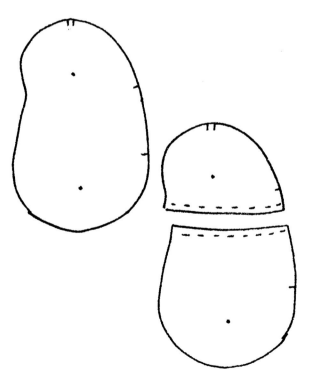

Arms different design options

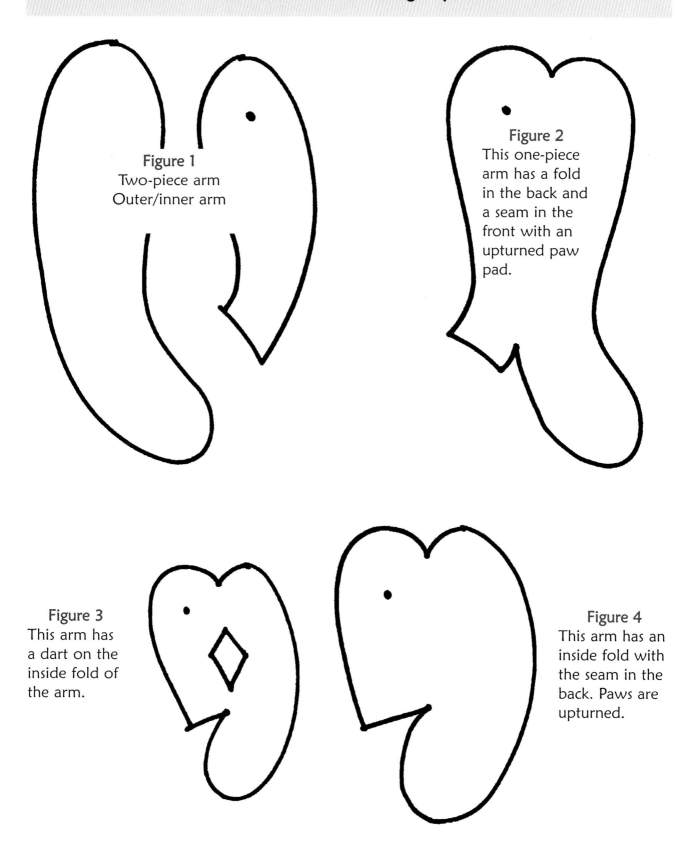

Figure 1
Two-piece arm
Outer/inner arm

Figure 2
This one-piece
arm has a fold
in the back and
a seam in the
front with an
upturned paw
pad.

Figure 3
This arm has
a dart on the
inside fold of
the arm.

Figure 4
This arm has an
inside fold with
the seam in the
back. Paws are
upturned.

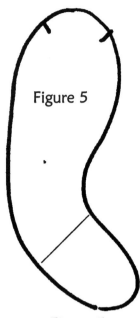

Figure 5

Figure 6

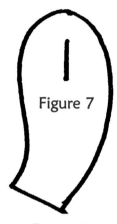

Figure 7

Figure 5
The opening for stuffing and jointing is on the rounded portion at the top of the arm. Leave the opening only large enough to slip in the joint.

Figure 6
The opening for stuffing and jointing is on the back side of the arm.

Figure 7
This option is used by many manufacturers as well as by some artists. The arm is sewn entirely around all the curves. Joint placement is calculated, and a slit is cut on the inside of the arm or on the side that has the paw pad. The arm is then stuffed, the joint is placed and the slit is ladder-stitched shut.

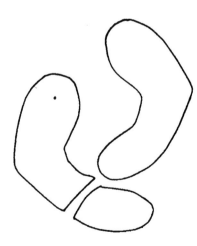

Figure 8
Bent arm paw up

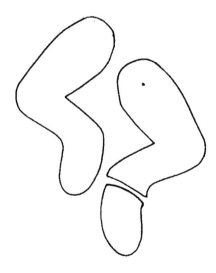

Figure 9
Bent arm paw down

Optional Arm

This arm is sewn in the same way as a regular arm, but designed to joint differently, creating an arm that rotates in front of the bear's body, instead of rotating along its side. This design can be used to create, for example, a ballerina with arms or toes pointing in or out rather than forward. Follow the diagram for further clarification.

Look at yourself in a mirror. Facing the mirror, move your arm up and down at the side of your body, as a bear's arm would rotate. Note the movement. Now standing in the same position, rotate your shoulder forward towards your chin with your arm bent at the elbow. Hold that position and move your arm—still bent at the elbow and rotated forward up and down. Note this movement. This arm design will create this kind of movement in your bear.

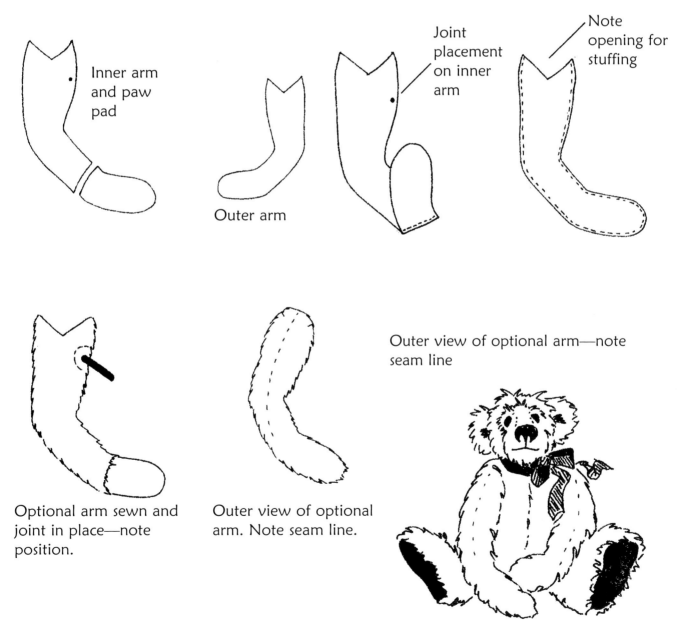

Inner arm and paw pad

Outer arm

Joint placement on inner arm

Note opening for stuffing

Optional arm sewn and joint in place—note position.

Outer view of optional arm. Note seam line.

Outer view of optional arm—note seam line

23

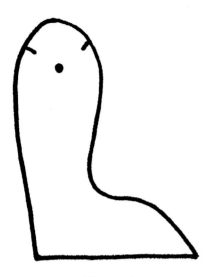

Figure 1
Two-piece leg, cut two;
cut two reversed.

Figure 2
One-piece leg, cut one;
cut one reversed.

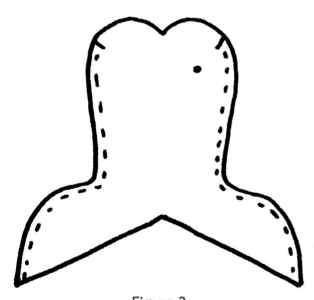

Figure 3
This design will tip the feet forward to
look as an old bear does when it is worn
and droopy. Cut one; cut one reversed.

Figure 4
Two-piece, bent-leg bear.
Cut two; cut two reversed.

Paw Pads shapes and how to make them

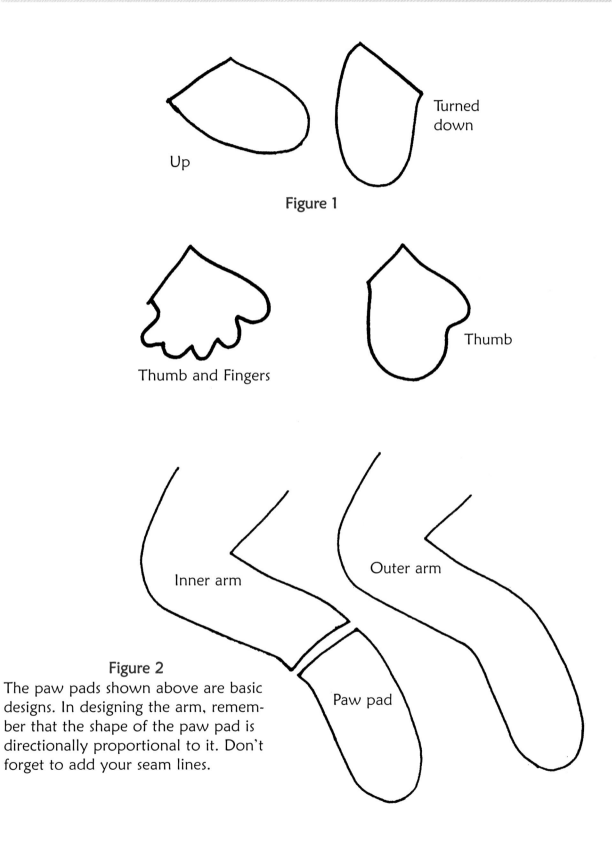

Up

Turned down

Figure 1

Thumb and Fingers

Thumb

Inner arm

Outer arm

Figure 2
The paw pads shown above are basic designs. In designing the arm, remember that the shape of the paw pad is directionally proportional to it. Don't forget to add your seam lines.

Paw pad

Foot Pads designing and different looks

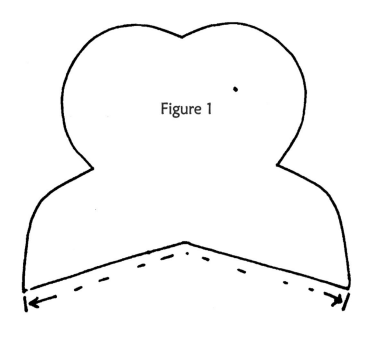

Figure 1

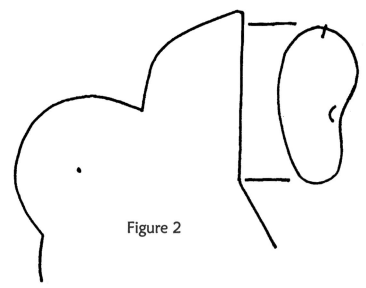

Figure 2

Figure 1
Here is one method for designing a foot pad.

Use a piece of string to measure from the tip of the toe along the bottom of the foot, continuing to the other side as shown. Lay the measured string on a sheet of paper and shape to the style you like.

Figure 2
This is one of the methods I use for designing a food pad. I draw a line at the heel, and a line approximately 1/4 – 1/2 inch down from the toe. I draw the shape freehand, adjusting the pattern as I work.

*Foot pads generally need adjusting as the fabric of the foot pad and that of the bear's leg are usually different from each other, especially as far the stretch and firmness of the two fabrics are concerned.

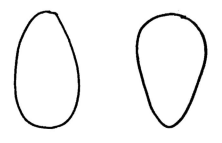

Figure 3
Different shapes

Tails or not to tail

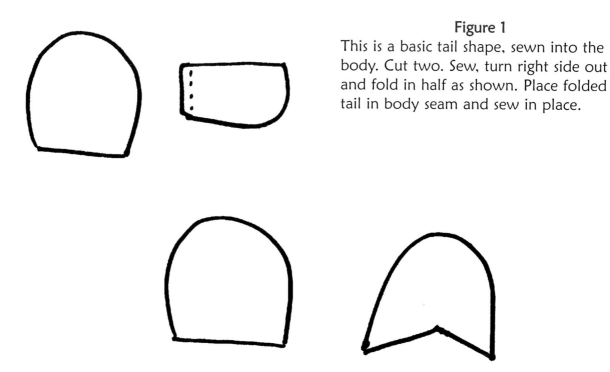

Figure 1
This is a basic tail shape, sewn into the body. Cut two. Sew, turn right side out and fold in half as shown. Place folded tail in body seam and sew in place.

Figure 2
To create this tail, cut one basic tail as shown on left, then cut one as shown on right. The underside of the tail has a dart. Sew the dart pin to the basic tail, sew, then turn it right side out. After stuffing the body, attach the tail, with cupped side down, to the body and sew in place.

Noses to smell or not

Figure 1

Figure 2
Noses are a matter of choice when it comes to size, color and type of yarn. Whether you back up the nose area with leather or with felt, keep stitching till the cows come home or use tacky glue, as I do, to hold the yarn in place, so it doesn't separate. Pictured are a few basic ways to stitch a nose. Use your imagination and create a style of your own.

Joint Placement sizes to use, drawing using a disk as a template, positioning joints

Figure 1 is a standard joint placement.

Figure 2 pulls the arms and/or legs forward, making the bear's arms and shoulders appear to be drawn forward, and the bear's feet appear to be pigeon-toed.

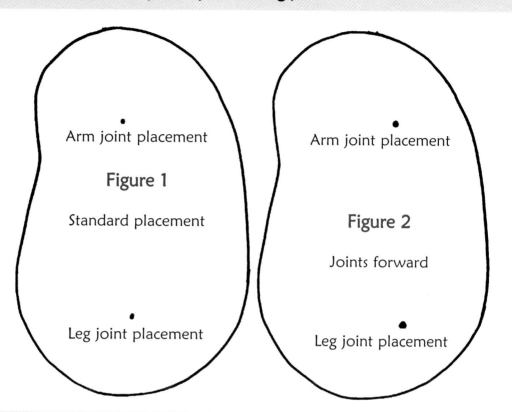

Arm joint placement

Figure 1

Standard placement

Leg joint placement

Arm joint placement

Figure 2

Joints forward

Leg joint placement

Joint sizes placement

Figure 3

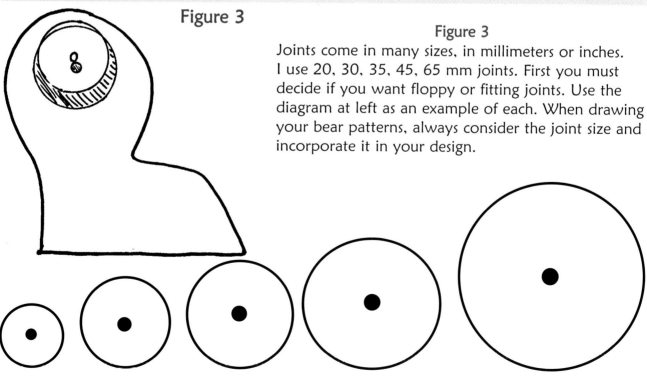

Figure 3
Joints come in many sizes, in millimeters or inches. I use 20, 30, 35, 45, 65 mm joints. First you must decide if you want floppy or fitting joints. Use the diagram at left as an example of each. When drawing your bear patterns, always consider the joint size and incorporate it in your design.

Stitches

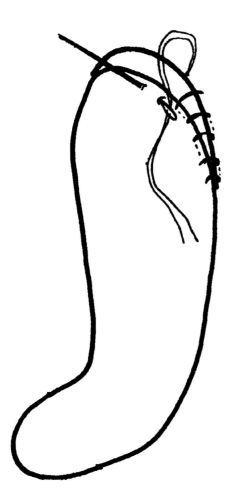

Figure 1
Ladder Stitch
Best for closing seams and
sewing on ears

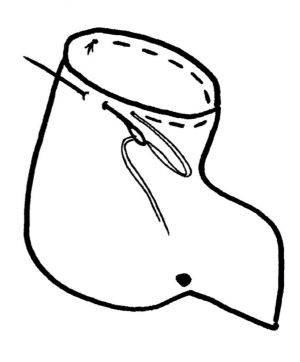

Figure 2
Gathering Stitch
(also called Running Stitch or Basting Stitch)
Used for drawing in the head around the neck
joint

Open Mouth

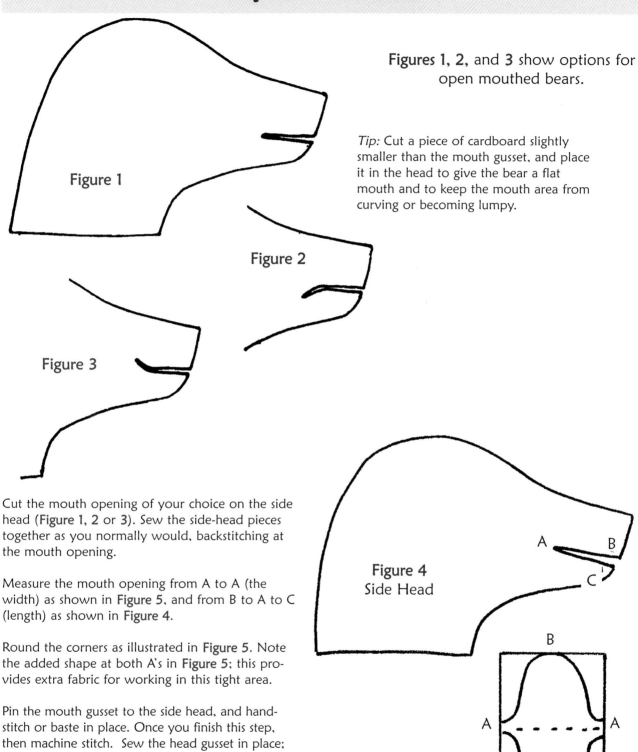

Figure 1

Figure 2

Figure 3

Figures 1, 2, and **3** show options for open mouthed bears.

Tip: Cut a piece of cardboard slightly smaller than the mouth gusset, and place it in the head to give the bear a flat mouth and to keep the mouth area from curving or becoming lumpy.

Cut the mouth opening of your choice on the side head (**Figure 1, 2** or **3**). Sew the side-head pieces together as you normally would, backstitching at the mouth opening.

Measure the mouth opening from A to A (the width) as shown in **Figure 5**, and from B to A to C (length) as shown in **Figure 4**.

Round the corners as illustrated in **Figure 5**. Note the added shape at both A's in **Figure 5**; this provides extra fabric for working in this tight area.

Pin the mouth gusset to the side head, and handstitch or baste in place. Once you finish this step, then machine stitch. Sew the head gusset in place; turn right side out and stuff; paying extra attention to the mouth area. Stuff lower mouth or chin lightly.

(These directions were developed with the help of Celia Baham of Celia's Teddies.)

Figure 4
Side Head

Figure 5
Mouth Gusset

Double-Jointed Head

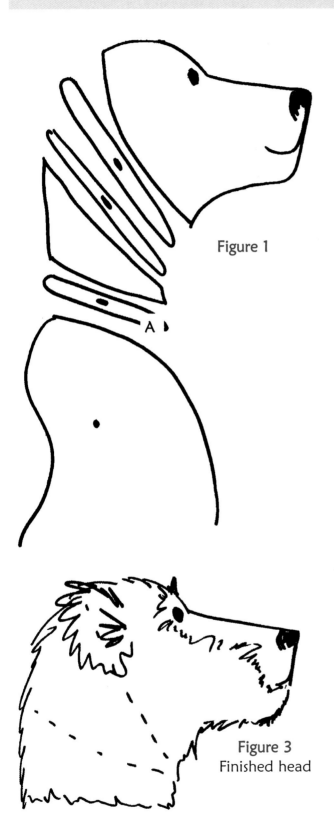

Figure 1

Figure 1 shows the pieces needed to double-joint a head. You may choose different angles. I find that the one pictured works best. In my opinion, this method is not useful for a production piece; I would use it only for creating limited editions or one of a kinds. But that is my personal opinion, due to a lack of patience!

After finding your angles (**Figure 2**) draw a circle 1/4 inch larger than the joint you will use. Note: if you don't work around existing sizes of joints you will have to make your own to meet your proportions. You will need two or three circles—two if you are using a gathering stitch around the bottom piece with the neck joint (see A in **Figure 1**).

Sew your pieces together, remembering to leave an opening for jointing and stuffing. Also take into consideration your head gusset. Don't forget to add your ¼-inch seams.

Figure 2
Two angles for joint placement are pictured in the drawing. Choose the one that meets your needs.

Figure 3
Finished head

Now, using the basics I have just shown you, let's make a bear!

Basic Directions

Read the directions carefully before you start. I will be referring to mohair or fur throughout the instructions. Plush furs are also acceptable. Most American plush is knit, not woven, and will stretch, such as knit sweaters do. Mohair and some European plush is woven; these have less give and don't stretch. Pattern pieces cut out of different fabrics will have different degrees of give or stretch. When using fabric other than mohair or plush for paw pads you may have to ease or pull to make the paw pad fit the leg piece.

I will also refer to "pile." This is the furry side of the fur. Pile comes in different lengths, thickness, densities. It can be straight, kinky, wavy, sparse... "Nap" or the direction of the nap is the way the fur lies smoothly when you pass your hand over it.

Cutting out your pattern pieces

Trace the pattern pieces onto cardboard. Cardboard pattern pieces are easier to trace around than paper. I use cardboard from tablet backs; it's sturdy but easy to cut with scissors. (*Talk to your local print shop and ask if you may purchase large uncut sheets from them.*) Cereal boxes are also great for making pattern pieces. Make sure you trace all the pieces you need to make the bear. Mark nap direction arrows, joint placement, head joint opening lines and openings for stuffing as well as center front marking on foot pads on to your cardboard pattern pieces. Cut out a small hole in the pattern pieces for joint placement (holes are marked on the original pattern; pieces with marked holes are the inner arm, leg and body).

Laying out your pattern on the mohair or plush and cutting

Remember to include the reversed pieces such as the side head, body, outer arm, inner arm, leg, paw pad, foot pad and ear. For example, when tracing the legs, which are identical, you need to reverse the pattern piece, changing the joint marking placement in order to have a right and a left leg.

Lay the mohair right side down (that means furry side down) in a single thickness. Note the pile direction and the arrow directions on the pattern pieces. The arrows will follow the nap or the way the fur lays smooth when you pass your hand over the fur. *Mohair nap does have a habit of changing directions; check often for changes as you trace your pattern pieces.*

Lay out your pattern pieces as close together as possible, paying attention to the nap and the direction of the arrows on the pattern pieces, to save on the expense of the mohair. Large and small scraps can go towards making another bear or, if you have made a mistake, you may have sufficient fabric to replace the mistake. Trace the pieces on to the back of the fur. Lay out your pattern. Trace using chalk pencils, permanent markers, liquid paper pens (correction pen) or any other means to identify your cutting lines and other markings important to the bear's pattern. Cut carefully using sharp scissors. Only cut the fur's backing, and not the pile. The fur's backing is the woven or knit base that the pile is attached to. This requires you to take small snips with the point of your scissors. If you cut the pile, it will show on your finished bear as shorter pile in and along the seam lines.

To pin or not to pin?

I pin all my pieces together before sewing—except my foot pad to the leg. I pin only the center front on the foot pad to the center front seam on the leg. Some artists can sew their pattern pieces together without the help of pinning, some tape or staple the pieces together, and the more meticulous baste the seams after pinning. I am comfortable with pinning; it is more time-consuming but, for me, it makes a better bear. In the beginning, pinning is best; as time goes by, you will develop your own methods. When pinning your pieces, push any mohair pile to the inside or trim your pile from the ¼-inch seam allowances. When I work with really long pile, I trim all my seam lines.

Tips / Thread

I generally add ½ inch to the back of the head-gusset pattern piece to allow for the use of woven mohair or knit plush. When you pin, if you have an extra-long gusset piece that extends beyond your side head—which some people refer to as a "tail"—cut it off. It's that simple.

All seams are ¼ inch and are included in the pattern piece, and noted with a broken line. I use a size 18 sewing machine needle made for sewing denim and heavy fabrics on my 1932 and 1951 Singer sewing machines. I also use small stitches and clear nylon interlock (serger) thread. Using this thread requires that you sew all your seams twice. Using this method results in stronger seams for pellet-filled bears. If you use clear nylon thread, you don't have to match thread color to mohair color. If you are planning to fill your bear with pellets, I recommend that you double-sew your seams no matter what thread you use. If you are just starting out, or your preference is regular thread, that's acceptable. Match your fur color as close as possible to the thread color, changing colors if the pattern piece color is different— for example, when making Vladimir's paws and coat (page 120).

After your seams are sewn and before you turn your body part right side out, carefully comb the fur pile caught in the seams to the inside. I use a metal dog comb. But be careful not to rip your seams when combing the fur caught in the seams. This assures a more finished natural look when you have turned your body part right side out. The seam line will be less noticeable. If you don't do this, there will be shorter mohair pile in your seam line and your bear will not have a smooth finished look.

After you have turned your body part right side out, comb any fur pile on the outside, which may be caught in the seam lines. This also helps create a smoother finished look with less noticeable seams and no short pile sticking out of the seam line. To relate this to something you just learned in the previous paragraph: you picked the mohair out of the seams on the inside—why not the outside?

Now let's start!

Side Head – Head Gusset

You should now have your pieces cut out with all the important markings on the backing of your mohair or plush pattern pieces. Pin the side heads, pile sides together; stitch the side head from the nose to the neck edge or opening. Comb the fur caught in the inside seam line.

Pin, then stitch the side-head pieces to the head gusset, starting at the nose and sewing to the neck edge. Do the same with the other side of the side head and head gusset. Comb your seams out on the inside. Turn the finished head right side out, comb the fur from the seam lines and set aside.

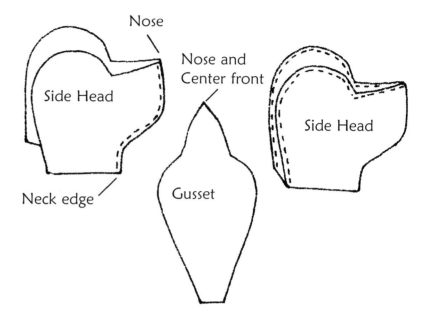

Ears

The ears in all the patterns in this book are two-piece ears, which means that you must cut two and cut two reversed. I am always cutting out more than one bear at a time so I mark my ears as X and O.

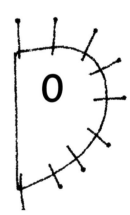

Bear Ears

Leave open for stuffing

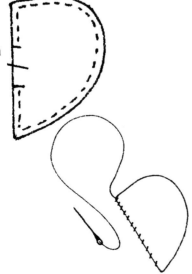

Pin an X to an O, and stitch the two pieces together. Repeat with the other ear pieces. Leave an opening for turning to the right side or the pile side in the center of the straight edge, as shown in the drawing. Turn both ears right side out and ladder-stitch the opening closed, leaving enough of the thread attached, as shown. Later you will stitch the ears on to the head, using the thread that is still attached to the ear. You will need enough length to attach and knot the ear to the head. Comb the seam lines and set aside.

Body

With right sides or pile sides pinned together, joint placement, head-joint placement and openings for stuffing marked on the fur backing, sew your pieces together, leaving the openings specified. *Hint:* at the head-joint opening and the opening for stuffing, back-stitch for added strength.

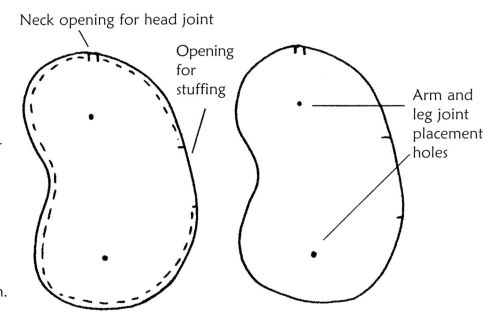

Before turning right side out, punch holes with the tip of a pair of CLOSED scissors or an awl at the joint placement markings. You will have four holes. Try not to break the threads while spreading the fur backing with the scissors or awl. Breaking the threads will create a weak spot on your bear. Do NOT cut a hole for placement of the joints. Note that your joint hole for the head joint is on your seam line. Comb seams on inside. Turn the body right side out; comb the seam lines on the outside and set aside.

Arms

With right sides together, pin, then stitch, inner arms to paw pads. The next step is to pin the completed inner arm/paw pad to the outer arm. Sew the two pinned pieces together, leaving an opening as marked at the top for stuffing and jointing. Repeat for the other arm. Punch holes for joint placement as you did for the body, using your scissors or awl. Comb pile from seam; turn right side out and comb pile from seam lines. Set aside.

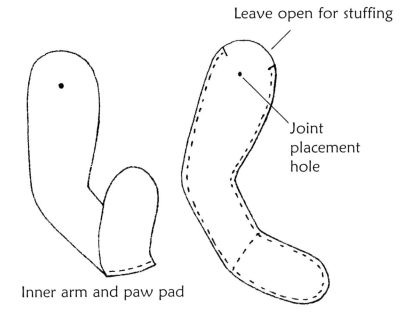

If you are making Dusty, Cal, Vladimir, Winston or Bubbles refer to the "Optional Arm" section on **page 23**, and follow the above directions.

Legs

With right sides together, pin, then stitch. Leave an opening at the top for stuffing and jointing, and at the bottom for the foot pad. Punch holes for joint placement with your scissors or awl. Remember you need a left and a right leg with corresponding holes. Comb seams. Do not turn right side out.

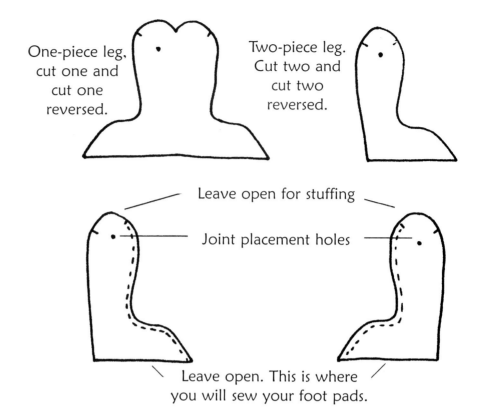

One-piece leg, cut one and cut one reversed.

Two-piece leg. Cut two and cut two reversed.

Leave open for stuffing

Joint placement holes

Leave open. This is where you will sew your foot pads.

Leg to Foot Pads

The foot pads in my newer designs are shaped something like a human foot, with a distinct left and a right. This means that when tracing the pattern piece you must reverse the piece to achieve this. The foot pad "arch" relates in shape to your feet, and the "arch" side is sewn onto the leg corresponding to the leg joint placement hole. See the drawing below.

Match the foot pad center front with the corresponding leg front seam; pin the foot pad to the bottom leg opening. Foot pads generally need adjusting as the fabric of the foot pad and that of the bear's leg are usually different, as is the give or stretch and firmness of the two fabrics. Repeat with the other leg and corresponding footpad. Turn right side out and set aside. Remember to comb your seams.

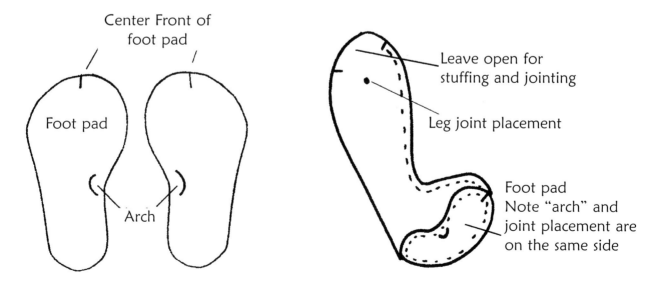

Center Front of foot pad

Foot pad

Arch

Leave open for stuffing and jointing

Leg joint placement

Foot pad Note "arch" and joint placement are on the same side

Finishing

Types of eyes

Now you've arrived at the final steps in finishing the bear. You will need your bear's head, and the eyes you have chosen. If you are using German glass or plastic eyes with a loop, hole or wire, at this stage you should stuff your head firmly to within ¼ inch of the neck opening. If you are using safety eyes read the following section about safety eyes.

Safety eyes

Safety eyes are commonly found in craft and fabric stores. If you use safety eyes, you must place them in the head before stuffing it. I use two pins with colored heads to mark the eye placement. You should put the pins through the head where you wish the eyes to be placed. Using your scissors or awl, punch a small hole where the pin is placed. Insert your eye shaft first and place the lock washer on to the eye shaft on in the inside of the head. Press firmly together. Now stuff the head, and continue on to the "Stuffing the Head" section and follow the directions.

German plastic and glass

If you are using German or Austrian eyes, you must first stuff the bear's head firmly to within ¼ inch of the neck opening. These eyes have a hole, loop or wire attached to them. Thread a three-inch doll needle (available at most fabric stores) with enough thread (at least 12 inches doubled) to go through the bear's head and come out the back of his head with enough extra to knot and bury the knot inside the head at the neck opening. I use upholstery thread (dental floss or other strong thread also works). Run the threaded needle through the eye hole or loop, and then separate the strands of thread and run the needle through the middle of these separated strands, drawing the knot down to the eye's loop or hole. Now follow the directions in the following section.

Safety eye and
lock washer

German plastic
eye with hole
in shaft

German
glass eye
with loop

German glass
eye on wire

Stuffing the Head, Attaching the Head Joint, and Eye Placement

There are many brands of stuffing. I use Quality A from **Monterey Mills** in Wisconsin, which, in my opinion, is the best. It is more expensive than others but it is well worth the money. It comes in 20-pound bags, feeds out in a coil and stuffs to perfection. There is less "fuzz" in this brand to float through the air and into your lungs.

Stuff the head to within ¼ inch of the neck opening; stuff firmly. (For Buckshot, Wilbur and Klondike you will need to stuff the muzzle firmly, taking special care where the muzzle narrows.)

Attaching the Head Joint

After you have stuffed the head, thread your needle with enough thread to do a running stitch around the neckline, and with enough length to whip stitch the neck opening closed around the head joint that will be placed in the neck opening. Sew your running stitch ¼ inch in from the edge. Refer to Stitches, **Figure 2**, on **page 30**. When you have your running stitches in place, place the joint you are using for the head into the neck opening. Refer to Jointing the head, arms and legs to the body on **page 41** for different kinds of joints available. The joint should be placed with the shaft side sticking out of the head. Draw in your thread tightly around the joint, whip stitch back and forth and around and across the neck opening, securing the joint in the head. Knot your thread.

Eye Placement

If you are using the German plastic or glass eyes, use pins with colored heads to mark their placement. Punch a hole with your scissors or awl in the spot you have chosen.

Thread your needle and attach the eye to it. Refer to German plastic and glass on **page 38** for instructions on thread and length. Run the needle through the eyehole and out the back of the bear's head. Pulling the thread tight and drawing the eye tightly and securely into the head, make a knot. Draw this knot back into the head and pull the thread out the neck line as close to the joint as possible; knot again. There are many ways of placing eyes, so feel free to use the one you are comfortable with.

Noses

I use wool DMC needlepoint floss for my noses. This is available at most craft stores. Other people use pearl cotton, which is used for embroidery, needlepoint or petitpoint. Pearl cotton comes in a #5, which is a finer or thinner grade used mostly for small bears, and in a #3, which is heavier and generally used for larger bears. Brand names abound; DMC and Anchor are most readily available through suppliers and craft stores. Pearl cotton comes in small "hanks." This is a weaving term, which brings me to offer you this tip: if you have a weaving shop near you see if they sell pearl cotton on a "cone." Some cones weigh about one pound—enough to last you a long, long time! Some people use only black. I say live a little—make your bear happy, and give him a colorful nose!

With the wool yarn, I use a double strand to stitch the nose and mouth. You may choose to use one color for the nose and another for the mouth or the same for both. If using colors other than black, color coordinate with the fur you are using. Nose style and placement is at the maker's discretion. Refer to Noses... to smell or not on **page 28**. Choose the style that suits you best or create a new one.

Ears

If you have followed my directions to this point and your bear's ears are turned right side out and stitched closed with the excess thread still attached, you are ready to give your bear hearing. There are many ways to attach ears; some have been described in the design section. Whatever works for you is the right way. Just be sure to sew them tightly to your bear's head, as some people insist on picking up a bear by his ears. Next time you reach for a bear's ear, think about how it would feel if someone picked you up in that manner.

Expression is a big factor in a bear's look, and ear placement can change the look of your bear as dramatically as eye placement. Changing the ear color, shaving the ear, or changing the direction of the nap on the ear, will all change your bear's appearance. When I am ready to place the ears I hold the bear's head in my lap with the face upturned. I then take the two ears and hold them to the head, moving them around to achieve the look or expression that suits me and the bear.

Early Ear

Now let's attach the ears. In my earlier designs, such as **Beasley, Vladimir** and **Cal**, the ears were shaped and attached to the head in a more normal manner. My newest ear design has a distinct shape and a way in which it must be placed on the head. This ear should be positioned down and towards the back of the head. Cup the ear forward. Sew the bottom half of the ear on at an angle and run the top half of the ear up the side head and gusset seam line. In simple terms, sew the ear on in a V shape. Examples of bears with these ears are Klondike and Buckshot.

Once you have decided on the placement and have the threaded needle attached to the thread on the finished ear attach the ear to the bear's head. Repeat for the other ear. You can use a ladder stitch, whip stitch or the "three stitch" ear method. Refer to Artists' Secrets for Making Better Bears on **page 142**. Comb the fur out around the ears. Your bear now has personality plus!

Directions for Jointing

Joint the head before you attach the arms and legs.

Follow the directions for the type of joint you are using, then attach the head as described in the following paragraphs.

There are many ways to joint a bear: cotter pins, plastic, lock nut and pop rivets are a few of the most popular. Some are sold with directions; some are not.

My opinion on jointing is to use what best suits you and the style of bears you design. Plastic works great for bears that are designed to be floppy or have a laid-back look. If you are looking for a very tightly jointed and "stiff" bear use lock nuts. Cotter pins tend to work loose as time goes by, but are probably the most often used. The cotter pins and lock nuts for making joints can be purchased through teddy bear suppliers or found at large hardware stores. Cotter pins come in different lengths and diameters.

When using any kind of joint, place the joint with the shaft end, cotter pin, bolt or pop rivet extending out of the head, arms and legs. The shaft will be placed through the holes you have punched for the head, arms and legs (as shown in the drawing below) and then into the body, using the jointing method of locking it tight inside the bear. Jointing must be done before the bear's body, arms and legs are stuffed.

Remember, joint the head to the body first!

Jointing the head, arms and legs to the body

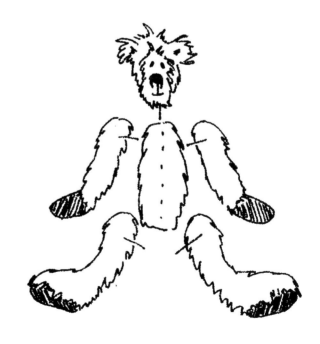

Plastic joints, cotter pins, lock nut or pop rivet joints are all attached differently. You will need five complete sets of joints to finish your bear. Remember your head-joint placement on the body is in the seam line. Regardless of which jointing method you use, follow the same jointing directions for the head as you do for the arms and legs in each joint description and method of attachment. Attaching the head first is recommended.

Make sure you have the body positioned in the right direction, with the body opening for stuffing at the front of the body. (In some patterns in this book the opening is in the back; the "back" is arched on the pattern piece.) Be sure the head joint opening is on top. Be careful to attach the arms to the armholes and not to the leg holes—it happens to the best of us sometimes. Joint sizes are listed in pattern requirements; you may also refer to Joint Sizes on **page 29**.

Plastic joints require for each joint: one joint with shaft attached, one washer and one lock washer for each completed joint. Using these joints, first place the joint with shaft attached through the bear's head, then through the corresponding arms and legs. The shaft should be protruding from the head, arms and legs as pictured in the previous drawing. Now that you have the joints in the head, arms and legs, place the shaft on the head through the body's head opening. On the inside of the body place the washer over the shaft, then place the lock washer (which has a raised ridge or slits in the center hole) onto the shaft. Press all the pieces together firmly to lock into place. Now attach the arms and legs in the same way.

Cotter pin joints require for each joint: one cotter pin, two metal washers (with a small opening hole so the cotter pin head won't pull through the washer), and two hardboard disks for each completed joint. You will also need a pair of needle-nose pliers to tighten and bend the cotter pins. Place the cotter pin through a metal washer, then through a hardboard disk. Then place this through the corresponding head, arm or leg holes. Insert the cotter pin so it is protruding from the head, arms or legs; now place the cotter pin into the body's head opening. On the inside of the body place a hardboard disk over the cotter pin, and then place the last metal washer over the pin. With your needle-nose pliers, separate and bend the cotter pin into a circular shape, so as to secure the joint tightly together. Now attach your arms and legs in the same way through the corresponding arm or leg holes. There are other ways of bending the cotter pin; use whatever works best for you.

Lock nut joints require for each joint: one bolt, one lock nut, two metal washers and two hardboard disks for each completed joint. You will need two wrenches or a wrench and a ratchet to tighten the bolt. First take the bolt and place a metal washer and then a hardboard disk on to the bolt. (If you are using this method for the head joint, glue the bolt head to the metal washer. You will not be able to tighten or hold the bolt in the head with your wrench because the head is stuffed and closed. Using this method on the head requires that you joint the head to the body before the head is stuffed.) Insert the bolt with the metal washer and hardboard disk attached into the corresponding arm or leg hole. Next place the bolt through the body's corresponding arm or leg holes. On the inside of the body, place a hardboard disk, and then a metal washer, onto the bolt. Next place your lock nut onto the bolt to tighten, using the wrench to hold the bolt head and the other wrench or the ratchet onto the lock nut.

Pop rivet joints require for each joint: one pop rivet, one metal washer and one hardboard disk for each completed joint. You will need a pop rivet gun for this joint. First place the hardboard disk onto the pop rivet, then insert the pop rivet into the body's corresponding arm or leg holes. On the inside of the body, place the metal washer over the pop rivet. Using your pop rivet gun, secure the joint. Now your bear is jointed and raring to go!

Stuffing... polyester, excelsior, plastic pellets, glass beads and steel shot?

The maker may choose from many different kinds of stuffing.

Polyester: I use 20-pound bags of Quality A Polyester from **Monterey Mills** in Wisconsin. Polyester stuffing is available through local fabric and craft stores in smaller bags and boxes.

Excelsior: This was used in the early manufactured bears, and is still used today. Some artists use excelsior in the form of fine shavings to stuff the end of the bear's nose or muzzle. They find this makes stitching the nose easier, and helps them achieve a firm and straight muzzle. I believe that if the nose or muzzle twists and doesn't come out straight, so be it. In my opinion, a twisted nose or muzzle adds more character to your bear's face. Excelsior can be used throughout the arms, legs and body.

Plastic pellets: I purchase plastic pellets in 1,000-pound quantities with a friend. We have it shipped in 50-pound boxes. You can purchase smaller quantities but the price is higher. I recommend that you get together with your friends or bear club members and order a large quantity. Call 00 info for **General Polymer,** a subsidiary of **Ashland Chemical,** to find a supplier close to you. Teddy bear suppliers also carry plastic pellets in smaller quantities for making just a few bears at a time.

Steel shot: can be purchased in small quantities from your teddy bear supplier or local sporting goods or firearms store. Steel shot is also used in sandblasting; it comes in different sizes and shapes from smooth and round to ruff. Do you have a sandblasting business in your area?

Glass beads: These are used commercially in highway construction—they are the shinny, sparkly little things in some road surfaces! Some teddy bear suppliers carry glass beads.

NEVER use lead shot!

When stuffing my bears I use only polyester in the head. I stuff the paws and feet, the neck area in the body and the bear's "bottom" with polyester. I stuff the remaining area in the arm, leg and body with plastic pellets. I use polyester at the top opening of the bear's arms, legs and tummy to hold in the pellets and give the body parts a rounded, smooth look when the openings are stitched shut. I use a ladder stitch for closing your seams. Refer to Stitches on **page 30**. Then I comb the fur from the seam lines, give my bear a bow, vest or just leave him naked.

Now sit back, enjoy this new little soul, and contemplate your next creation. Don't wait too long—even bears with human love and companionship get lonely for one of their own.

Beasley

Beasley

is 14" tall (roughly 35.5 cm)
and fully jointed.

Beasley appears on the cover of
The Teddy Bear Sourcebook
by **Betterway Books**

MATERIALS

- 1/4 yard (30" x 18") mohair; your choice style, color and length *1/4 yard measuring 9" x 58" is NOT suitable because of fabric requirements for arm/leg lengths*
- 9" square of velour upholstery fabric, felt, ultra suede or other fabric for paw pads
- One pair 9 mm glass or plastic eyes
- 3 sets – 35 mm joints for head and arms, 2 sets - 45 mm joints for the legs

- Yarn for nose and mouth.
- Sewing machine thread for seams to match mohair color (If you are stuffing with pellets, I recommend you sew all seams twice.)
- Nylon upholstery thread for attaching eyes and closing seams (this is what I use)
- Stuffing and plastic pellets

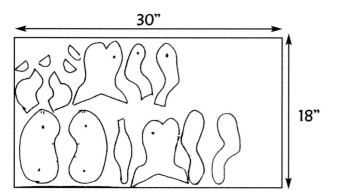

1/4 yard (30" x 18")

1/4 yard measuring 9" x 58" is NOT suitable because of fabric requirements for the arms/legs.

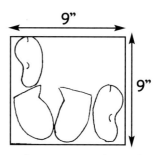

9-inch square for paw pads and foot pads

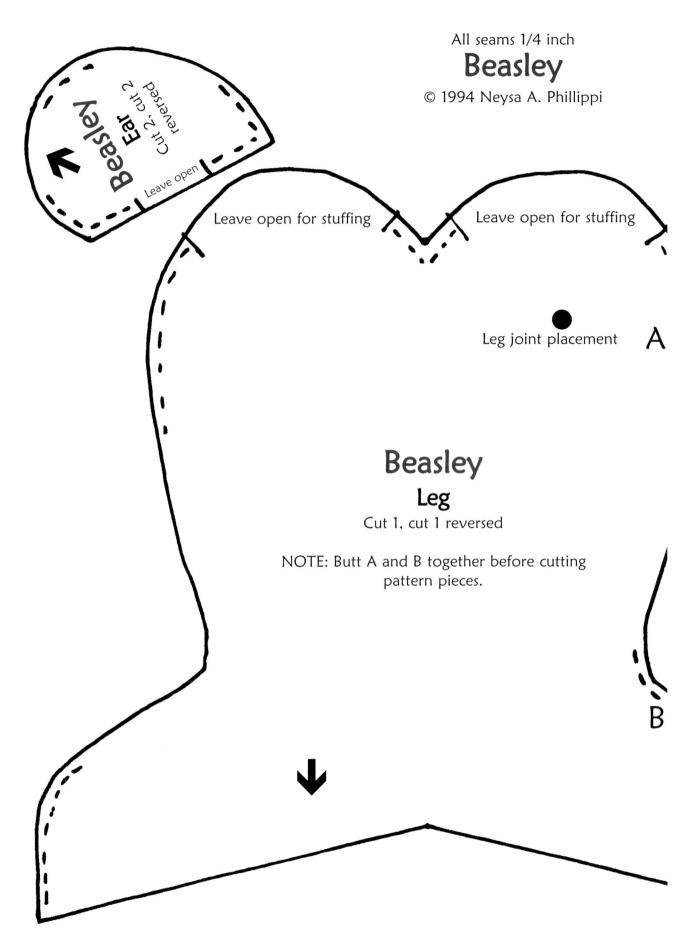

All seams 1/4 inch
Beasley
© 1994 Neysa A. Phillippi

Beasley
Ear
Cut 2, cut 2
reversed

Leave open

Leave open for stuffing

Leave open for stuffing

Leg joint placement

A

Beasley
Leg
Cut 1, cut 1 reversed

NOTE: Butt A and B together before cutting pattern pieces.

B

46

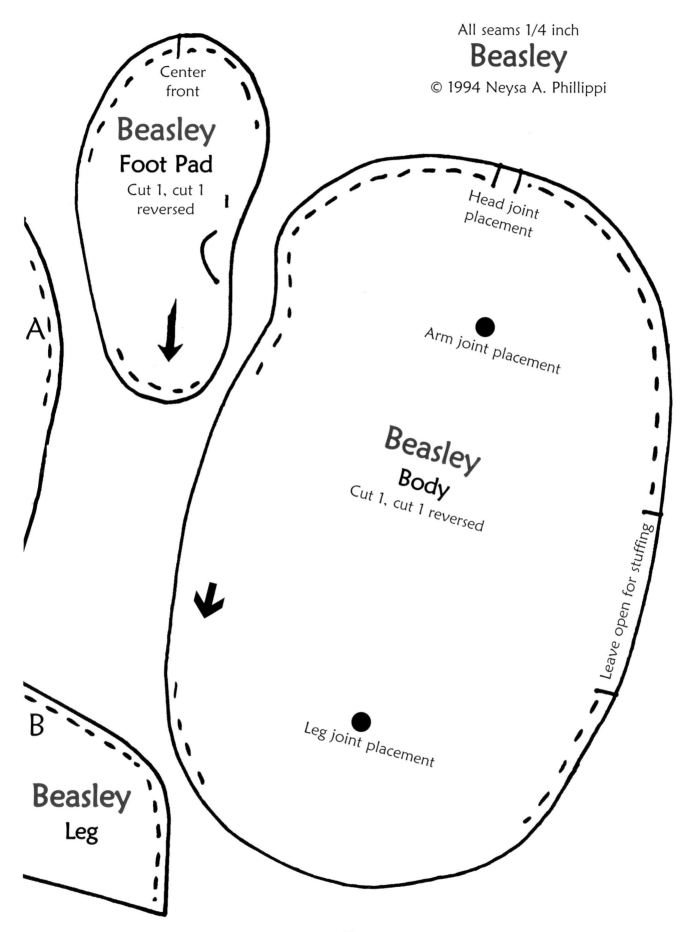

All seams 1/4 inch
Beasley
© 1994 Neysa A. Phillippi

Center front

Beasley
Foot Pad
Cut 1, cut 1 reversed

A

Head joint placement

Arm joint placement

Beasley
Body
Cut 1, cut 1 reversed

Leave open for stuffing

B

Beasley
Leg

Leg joint placement

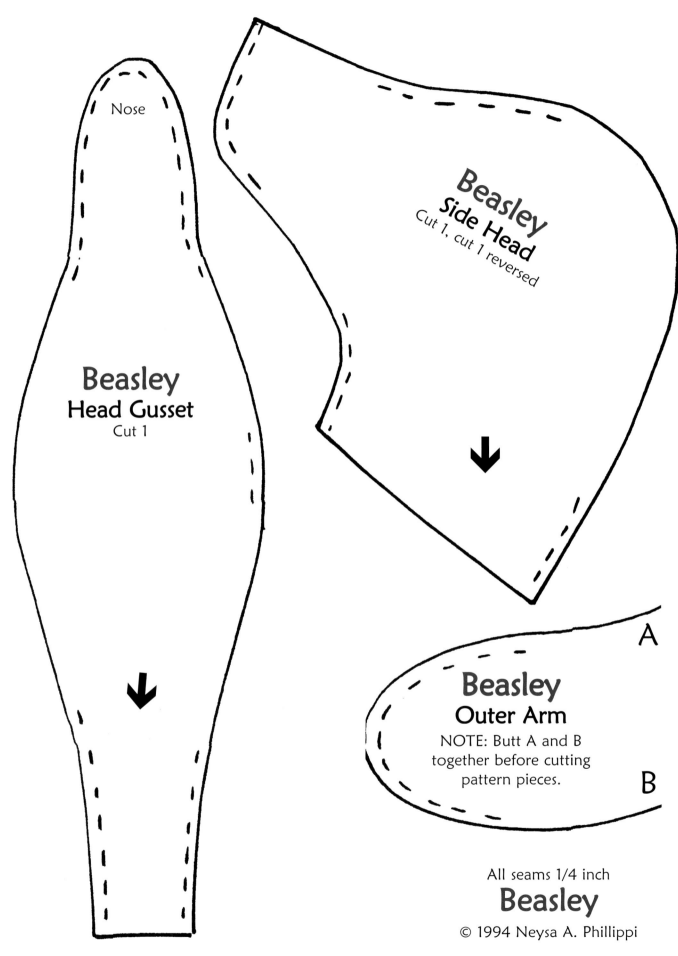

Nose

Beasley
Head Gusset
Cut 1

Beasley
Side Head
Cut 1, cut 1 reversed

A

Beasley
Outer Arm
NOTE: Butt A and B together before cutting pattern pieces.

B

All seams 1/4 inch
Beasley

© 1994 Neysa A. Phillippi

48

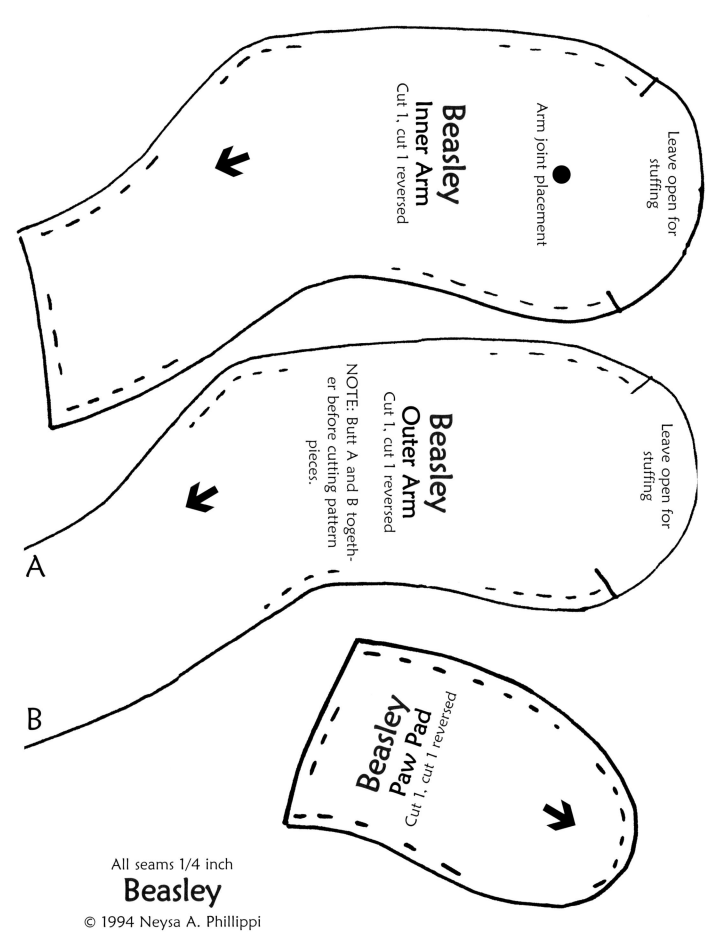

Beasley
Inner Arm
Cut 1, cut 1 reversed

Arm joint placement

Leave open for stuffing

A

B

NOTE: Butt A and B together before cutting pattern pieces.

Beasley
Outer Arm
Cut 1, cut 1 reversed

Leave open for stuffing

Beasley
Paw Pad
Cut 1, cut 1 reversed

All seams 1/4 inch
Beasley
© 1994 Neysa A. Phillippi

49

Bubbles

Bubbles

is 10" tall (roughly 25.5 cm) and
fully jointed and designed
to lie down.

MATERIALS

- 1/4 yard (30" x 18") OR 1/4 yard (9" x 58") mohair; your choice style, color and length
- 9" square of velour upholstery fabric, felt, ultra suede or other fabric for paw pads
- One pair 8 mm glass or plastic eyes
- 5 sets – 30 mm joints for head, arms, and legs
- Yarn for nose and mouth
- Sewing machine thread for seams to match mohair color (If you are stuffing with pellets, I recommend you sew all seams twice.)
- Nylon upholstery thread for attaching eyes and closing seams (this is what I use)
- Stuffing and plastic pellets

*** **Read Optional Arm** on page 23; this is the arm used for Bubbles.

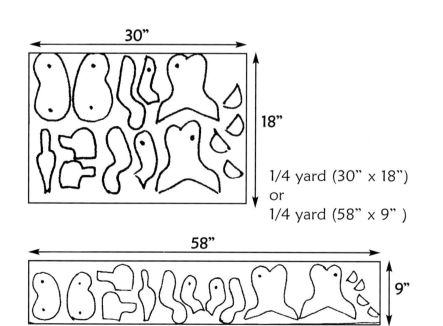

30"

18"

1/4 yard (30" x 18")
or
1/4 yard (58" x 9")

58"

9"

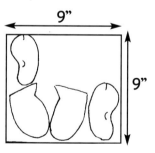

9"

9"

9-inch square for paw pads
and foot pads

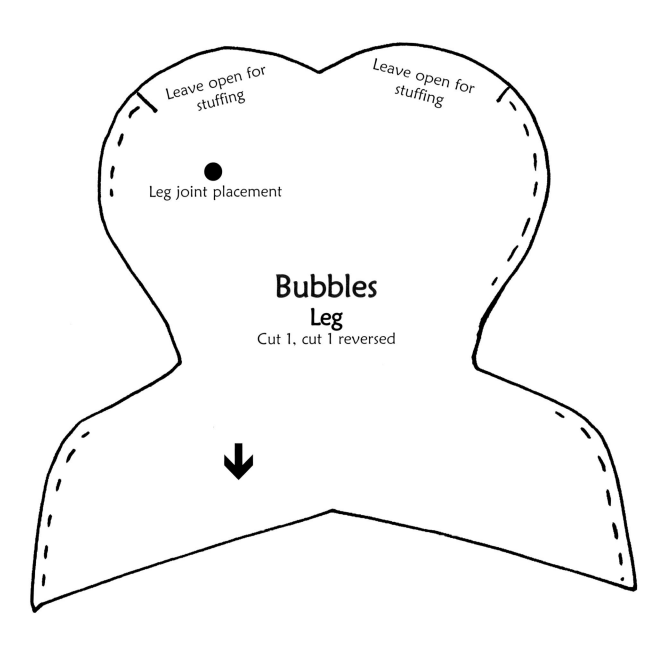

Leave open for stuffing

Leave open for stuffing

Leg joint placement

Bubbles
Leg
Cut 1, cut 1 reversed

All seams 1/4 inch
Bubbles
© 1995 Neysa A. Phillippi

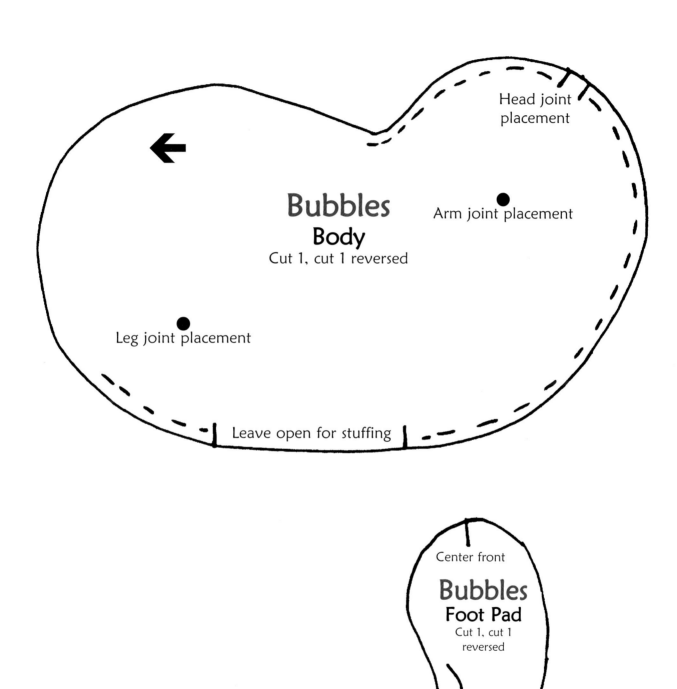

Head joint
placement

Bubbles
Body
Cut 1, cut 1 reversed

Arm joint placement

Leg joint placement

Leave open for stuffing

Center front

Bubbles
Foot Pad
Cut 1, cut 1
reversed

All seams 1/4 inch
Bubbles
© 1995 Neysa A. Phillippi

53

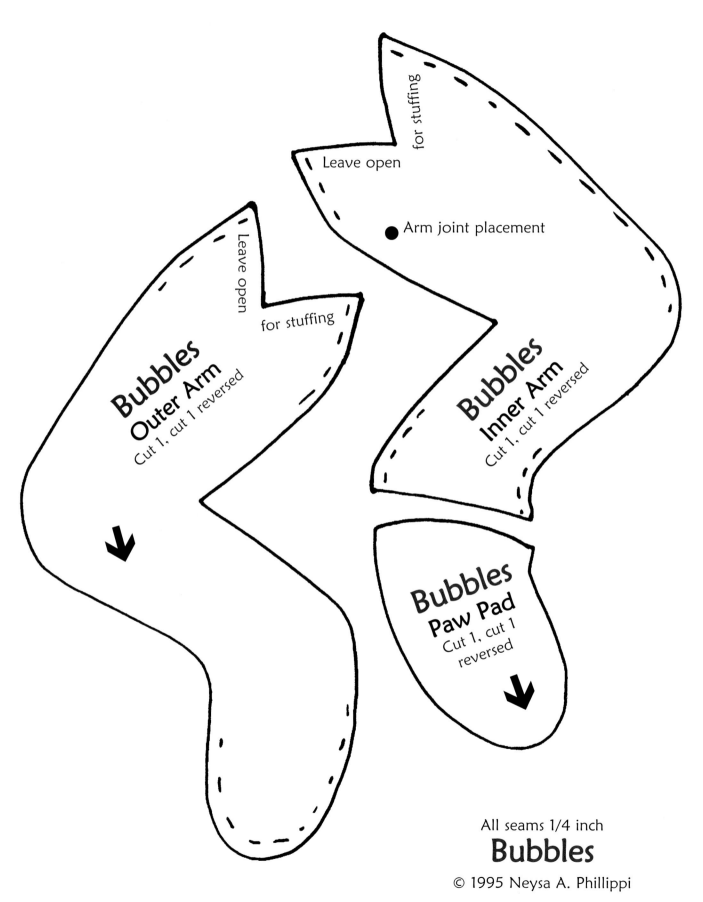

Leave open

for stuffing

● Arm joint placement

Leave open

for stuffing

Bubbles
Outer Arm
Cut 1, cut 1 reversed

Bubbles
Inner Arm
Cut 1, cut 1 reversed

Bubbles
Paw Pad
Cut 1, cut 1
reversed

All seams 1/4 inch
Bubbles
© 1995 Neysa A. Phillippi

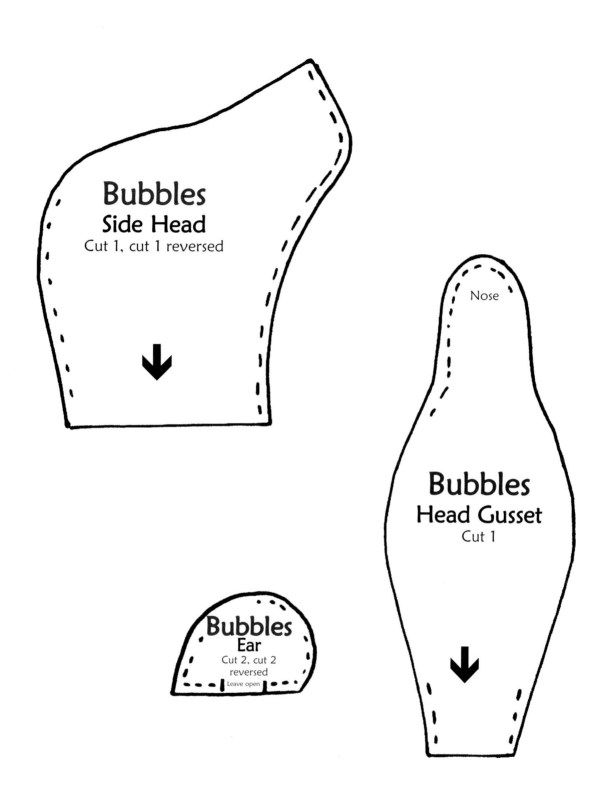

Bubbles
Side Head
Cut 1, cut 1 reversed

Nose

Bubbles
Head Gusset
Cut 1

Bubbles
Ear
Cut 2, cut 2
reversed
Leave open

All seams 1/4 inch

Bubbles

© 1995 Neysa A. Phillippi

Buckshot

Buckshot

is 17" tall (roughly 43 cm) and
fully jointed.

MATERIALS

- 1/2 yard (36" x 30") mohair, your choice style, color and length
- 9" square of velour upholstery fabric, felt, ultra suede or other fabric for paw pads
- One pair 9 mm glass or plastic eyes
- 3 sets – 35 mm joints for head and arms, 2 sets – 45 mm joints for the legs
- Yarn for nose and mouth

- Sewing machine thread for seams to match mohair color (If you are stuffing with pellets, I recommend you sew all seams twice.)
- Nylon upholstery thread for attaching eyes and closing seams (this is what I use)
- Stuffing and plastic pellets

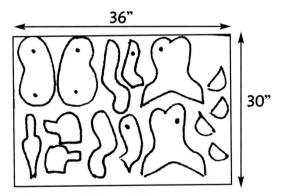

1/2 yard (36" x 30")

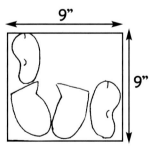

9-inch square for paw pads and foot pads

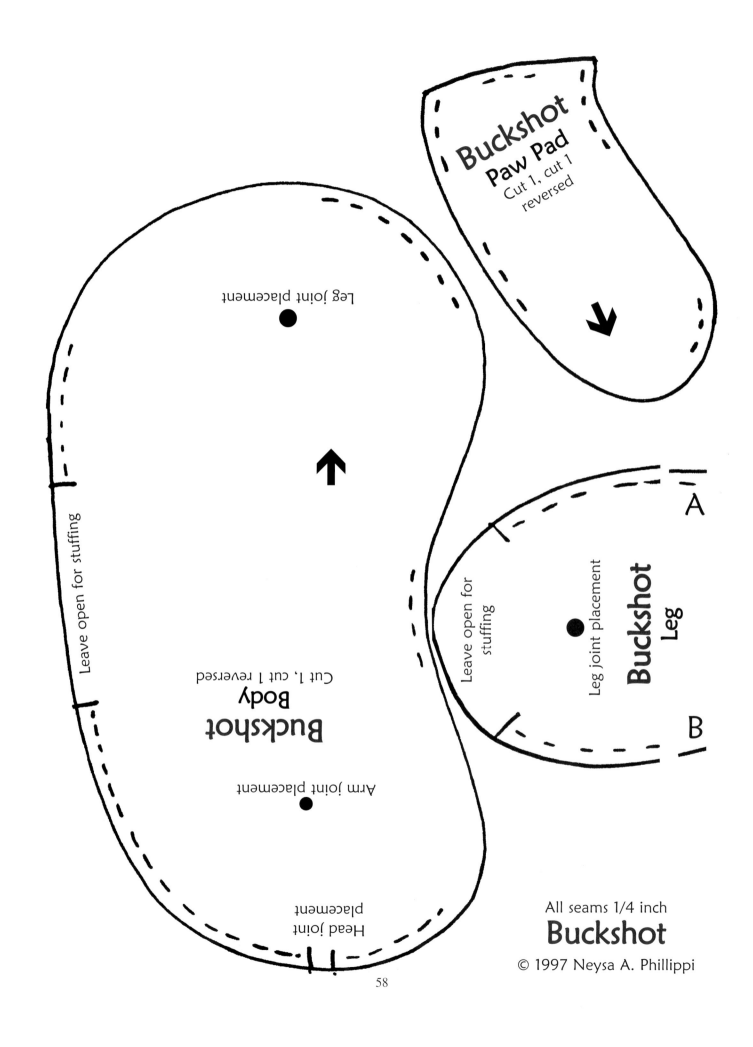

Buckshot
Paw Pad
Cut 1, cut 1 reversed

Leg joint placement

Buckshot
Body
Cut 1, cut 1 reversed

Leave open for stuffing

Arm joint placement

Head joint placement

Leave open for stuffing

A

Buckshot
Leg

Leg joint placement

B

All seams 1/4 inch
Buckshot
© 1997 Neysa A. Phillippi

58

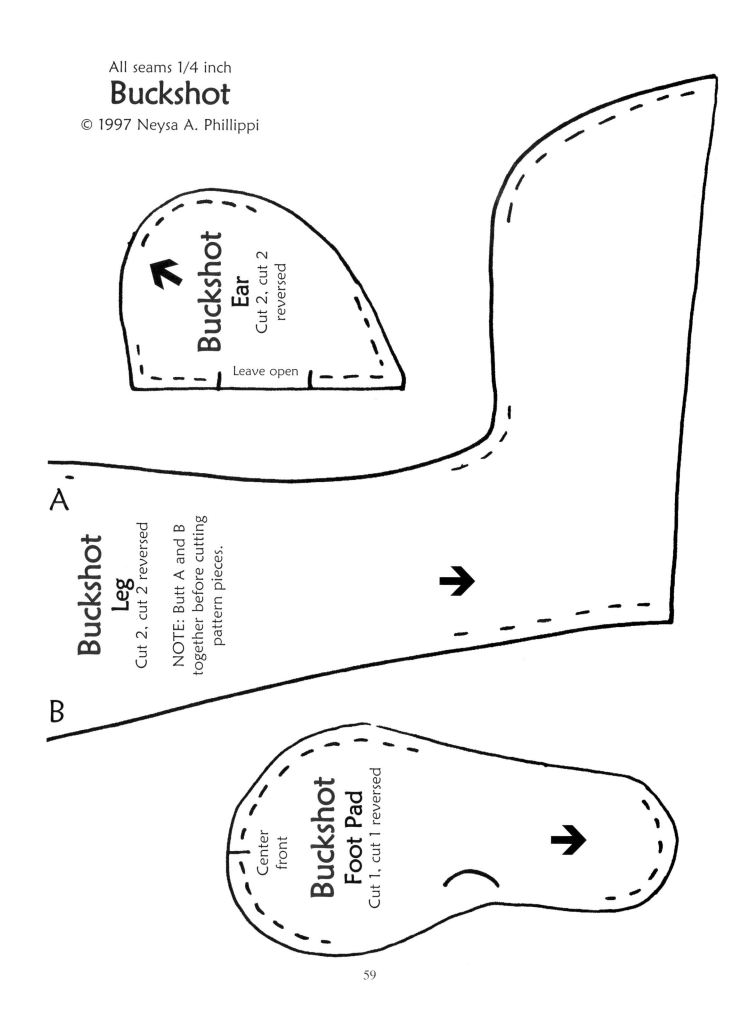

All seams 1/4 inch

Buckshot

© 1997 Neysa A. Phillippi

Buckshot
Ear
Cut 2, cut 2 reversed

Leave open

A

Buckshot
Leg
Cut 2, cut 2 reversed

NOTE: Butt A and B together before cutting pattern pieces.

B

Buckshot
Foot Pad
Cut 1, cut 1 reversed

Center front

59

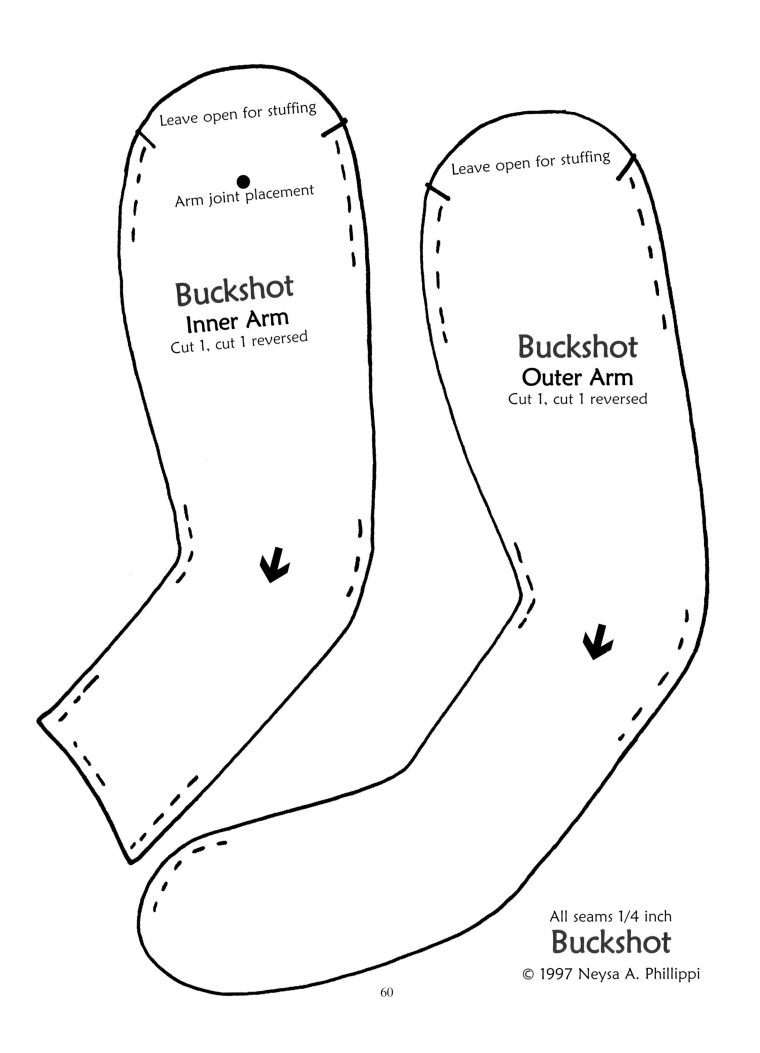

Leave open for stuffing

Arm joint placement

Buckshot
Inner Arm
Cut 1, cut 1 reversed

Leave open for stuffing

Buckshot
Outer Arm
Cut 1, cut 1 reversed

All seams 1/4 inch
Buckshot
© 1997 Neysa A. Phillippi

60

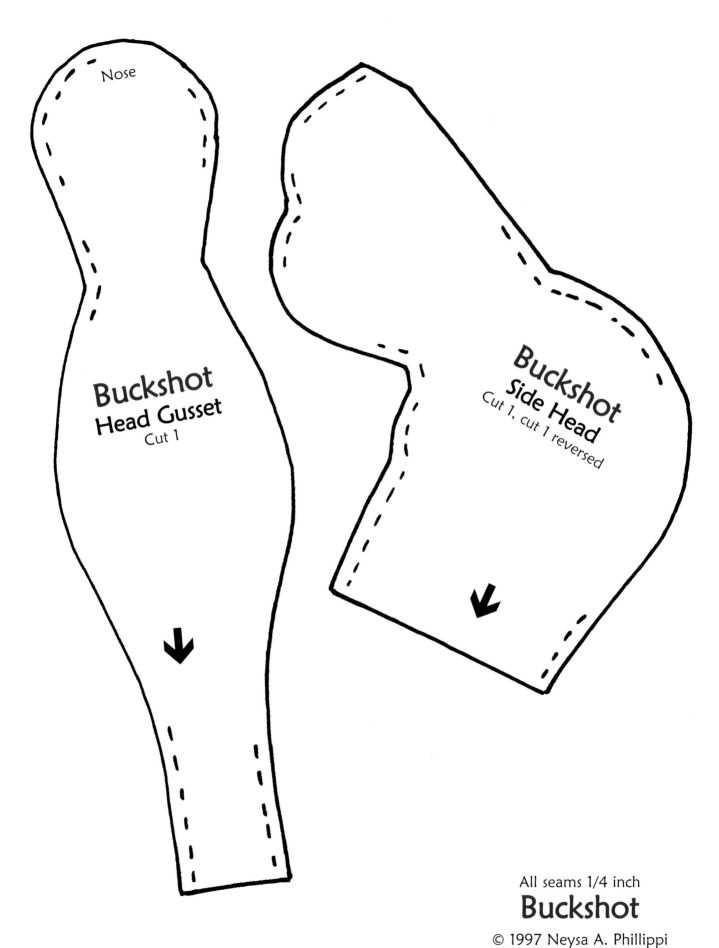

Nose

Buckshot
Head Gusset
Cut 1

Buckshot
Side Head
Cut 1, cut 1 reversed

All seams 1/4 inch
Buckshot
© 1997 Neysa A. Phillippi

Bumble

Bumble

is 12" tall (roughly 30.5 cm).

MATERIALS

- 1/4 yard (30" x 18") OR 1/8 yard (9" x 58") mohair, your choice style, color and length
- 9" square of velour upholstery fabric, felt, ultra suede or other fabric for paw pads
- One pair 9mm glass or plastic eyes
- 5 sets – 30mm joints for head, arms and for the legs

- Yarn for nose and mouth
- Sewing machine thread for seams to match mohair color (If you are stuffing with pellets, I recommend you sew all seams twice.)
- Nylon upholstery thread for attaching eyes and closing seams (this is what I use)
- Stuffing and plastic pellets

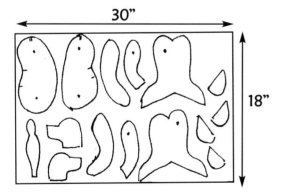

30"

18"

1/4 yard (30" x 18")
or
1/8 yard (9" x 58")

*** Layout shown uses straight arms; position Bumble's arms in same manner

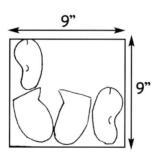

9"

9"

9-inch square for paw pads and foot pads

63

All seams 1/4 inch
Bumble
© 1994 Neysa A. Phillippi

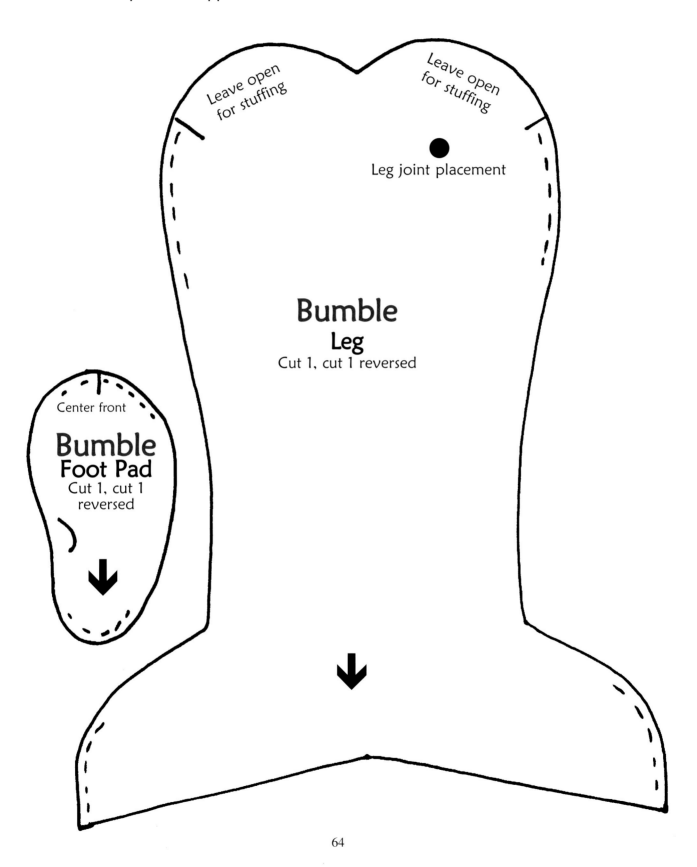

Leave open for stuffing

Leave open for stuffing

● Leg joint placement

Bumble
Leg
Cut 1, cut 1 reversed

Center front

Bumble
Foot Pad
Cut 1, cut 1 reversed

64

All seams 1/4 inch
Bumble
© 1994 Neysa A. Phillippi

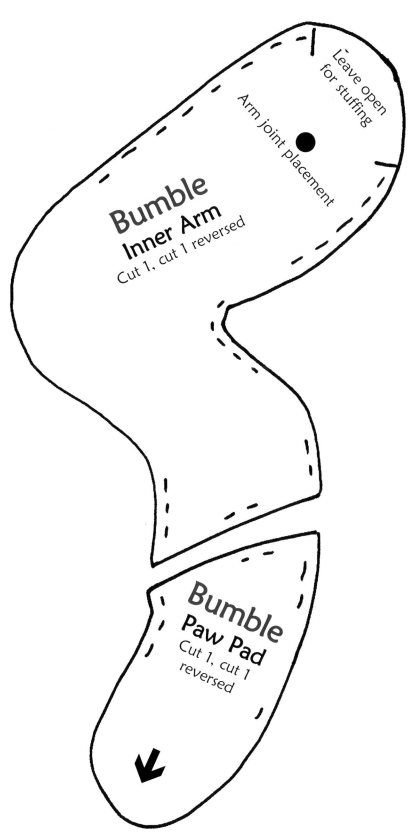

Leave open for stuffing

Arm joint placement

Bumble
Inner Arm
Cut 1, cut 1 reversed

Bumble
Paw Pad
Cut 1, cut 1 reversed

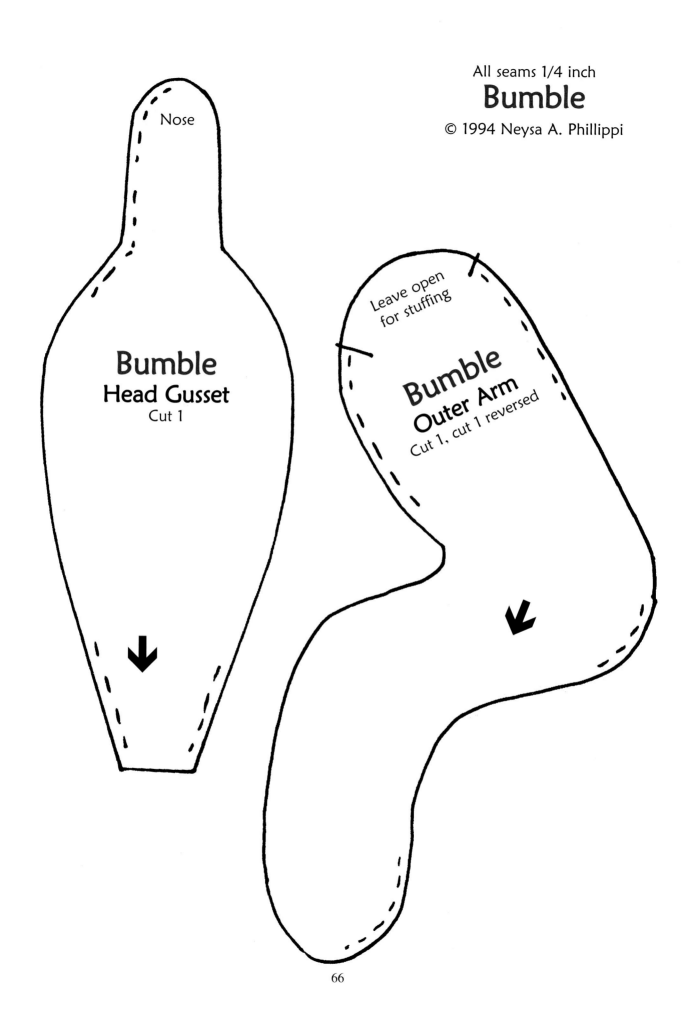

All seams 1/4 inch
Bumble
© 1994 Neysa A. Phillippi

Nose

Bumble
Head Gusset
Cut 1

Leave open
for stuffing

Bumble
Outer Arm
Cut 1, cut 1 reversed

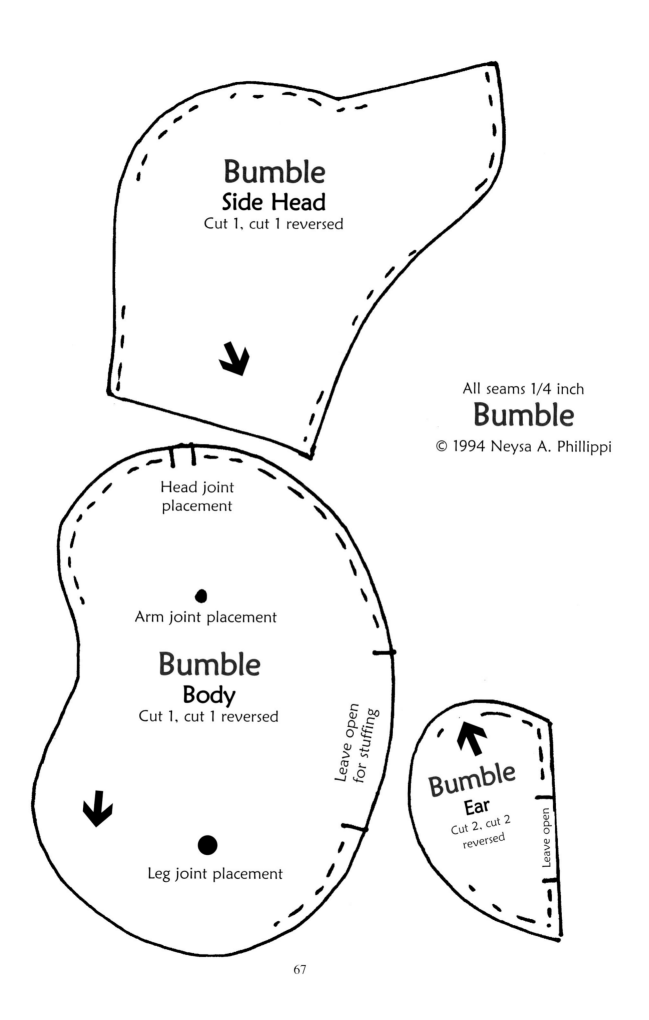

Bumble
Side Head
Cut 1, cut 1 reversed

All seams 1/4 inch
Bumble
© 1994 Neysa A. Phillippi

Head joint
placement

Arm joint placement

Bumble
Body
Cut 1, cut 1 reversed

Leave open
for stuffing

Leg joint placement

Bumble
Ear
Cut 2, cut 2
reversed

Leave open

67

Cal

Cal

is 15" tall (roughly 38 cm) and fully jointed.

MATERIALS

- 1/4 yard (30" x 18") mohair, your choice style, color and length *1/4 yard measuring 9" x 58" is NOT suitable; the arms/legs require more length*
- 9" square of velour upholstery fabric, felt, ultra suede or other fabric for paw pads
- One pair 9 mm glass or plastic eyes.
- 3 sets – 35 mm joints for head and arms, 2 sets – 45 mm joints for the legs

- Yarn for nose and mouth
- Sewing machine thread for seams to match mohair color (If you are stuffing with pellets, I recommend you sew all seams twice.)
- Nylon upholstery thread for attaching eyes and closing seams (this is what I use)
- Stuffing and plastic pellets

*** **Read Optional Arm** on page 23; this is the arm used for Cal.

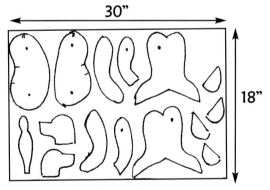

1/4 yard (30" x 18")

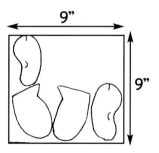

9-inch square for paw pads and foot pads

1/4 yard piece of fabric measuring 9" x 58" is NOT suitable; the arms/legs require more than the 9" length.

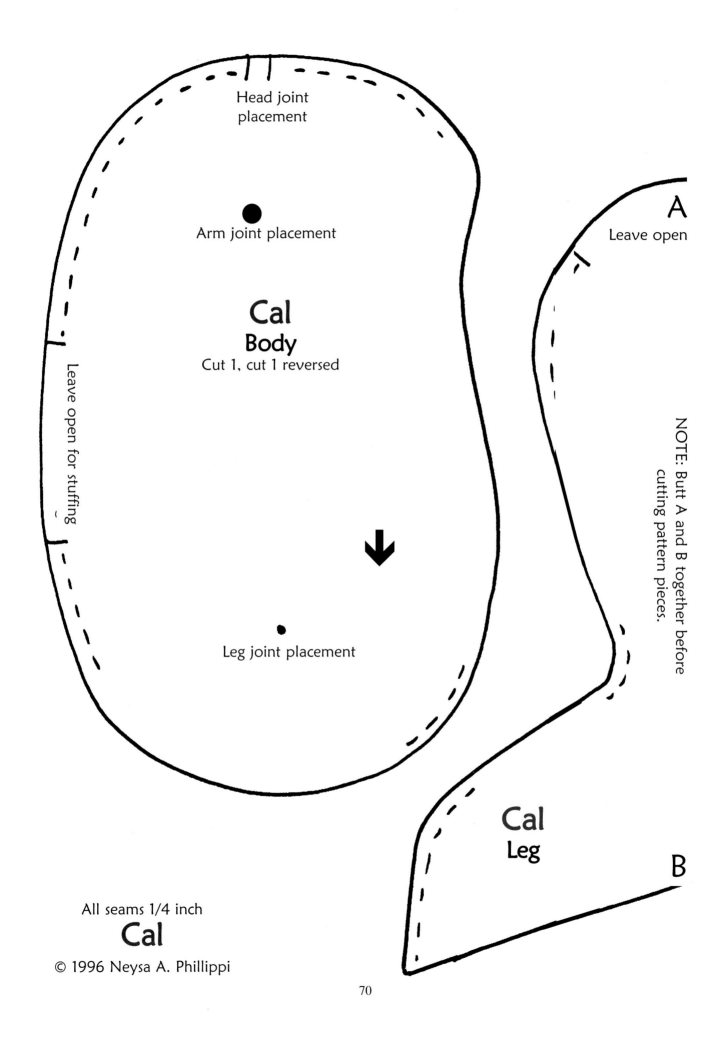

Head joint
placement

Arm joint placement

A

Leave open

Cal
Body
Cut 1, cut 1 reversed

Leave open for stuffing

NOTE: Butt A and B together before
cutting pattern pieces.

Leg joint placement

Cal
Leg

All seams 1/4 inch
Cal

© 1996 Neysa A. Phillippi

B

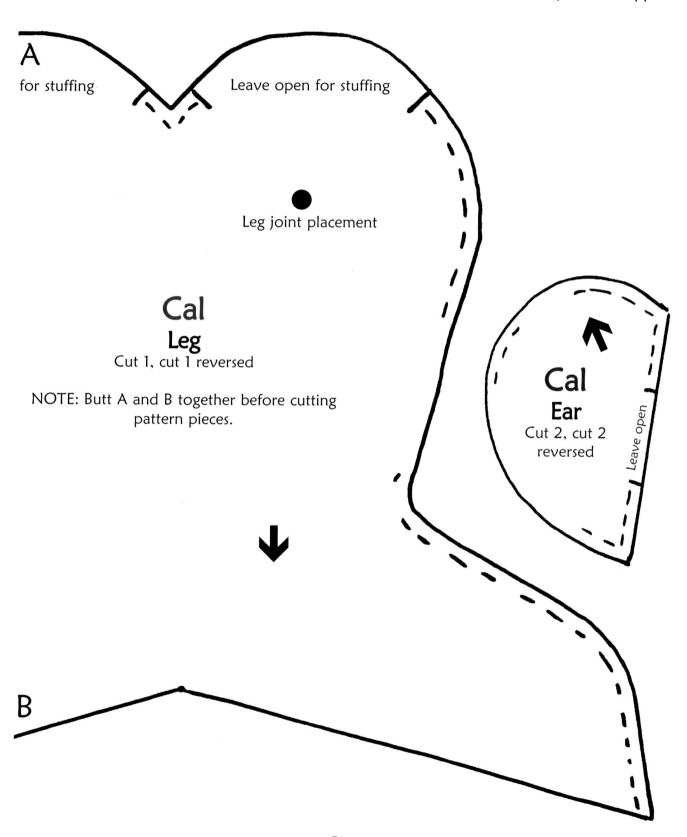

All seams 1/4 inch
Cal
© 1996 Neysa A. Phillippi

A

for stuffing

Leave open for stuffing

● Leg joint placement

Cal
Leg
Cut 1, cut 1 reversed

NOTE: Butt A and B together before cutting pattern pieces.

Cal
Ear
Cut 2, cut 2 reversed

Leave open

B

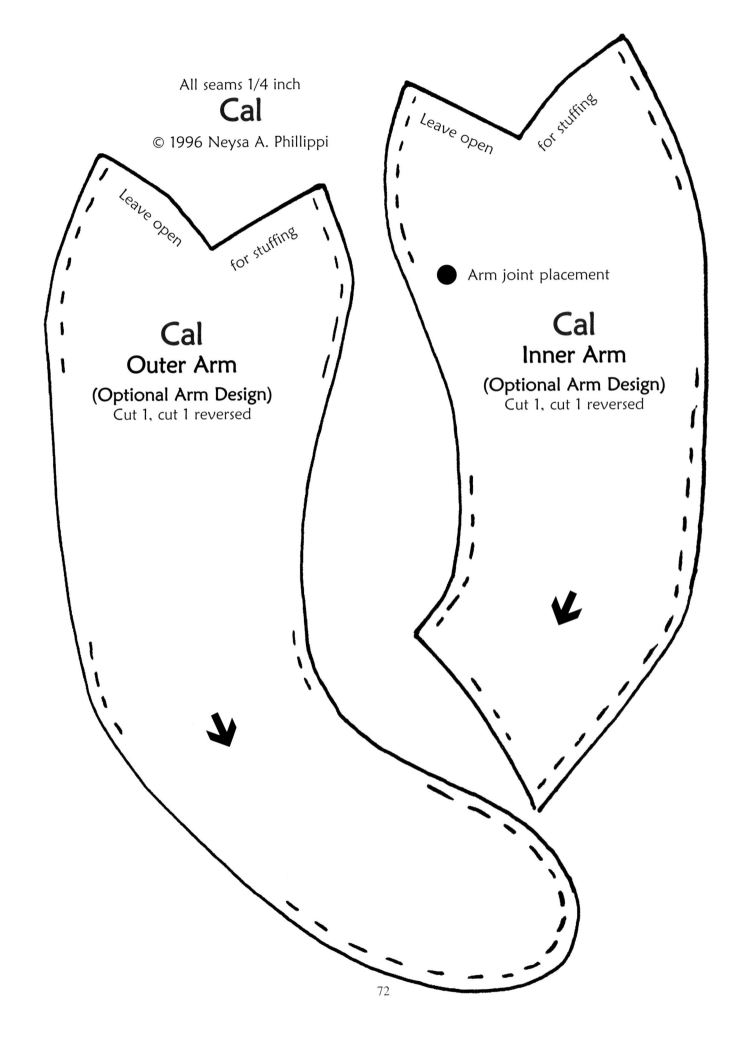

All seams 1/4 inch
Cal
© 1996 Neysa A. Phillippi

Leave open for stuffing

Cal
Outer Arm
(Optional Arm Design)
Cut 1, cut 1 reversed

Leave open for stuffing

● Arm joint placement

Cal
Inner Arm
(Optional Arm Design)
Cut 1, cut 1 reversed

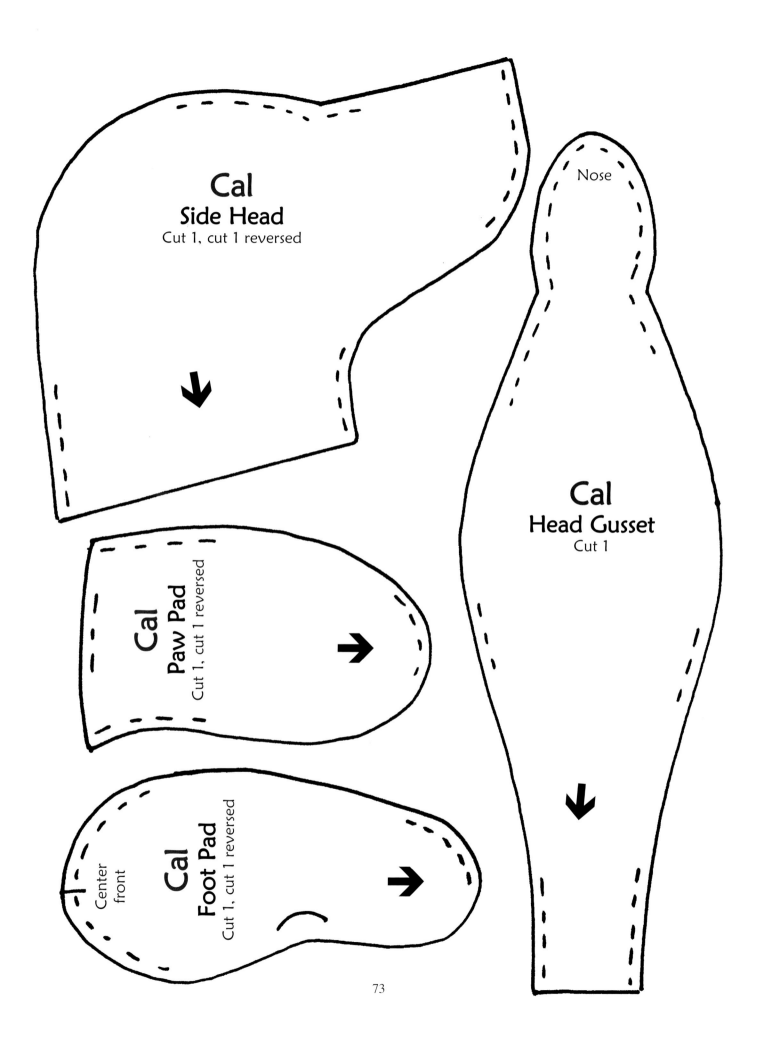

Cal
Side Head
Cut 1, cut 1 reversed

Nose

Cal
Head Gusset
Cut 1

Cal
Paw Pad
Cut 1, cut 1 reversed

Cal
Foot Pad
Cut 1, cut 1 reversed

Center front

73

Dusty

Dusty

is 12" tall (roughly 30.5 cm) and
fully jointed.

MATERIALS

- 1/4 yard (9" x 58") OR 1/4 yard (30" x 18") mohair, your choice style, color and length
- 9" square of velour upholstery fabric, felt, ultra suede or other fabric for paw pads
- One pair 9 mm glass or plastic eyes.
- 5 sets – 30 mm joints for head, arms and for the legs
- Yarn for nose and mouth

- Sewing machine thread for seams to match mohair color (If you are stuffing with pellets, I recommend you sew all seams twice.)
- Nylon upholstery thread for attaching eyes and closing seams (this is what I use)
- Stuffing and plastic pellets

*** **Read Optional Arm** on page 23; this is the arm used for Dusty.

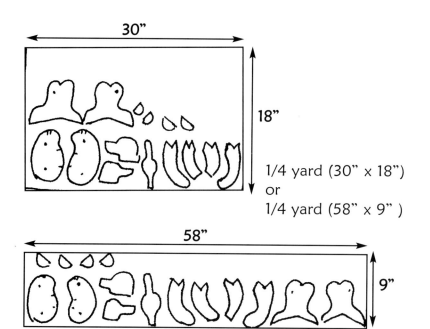

1/4 yard (30" x 18")
or
1/4 yard (58" x 9")

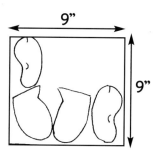

9-inch square for paw pads
and foot pads

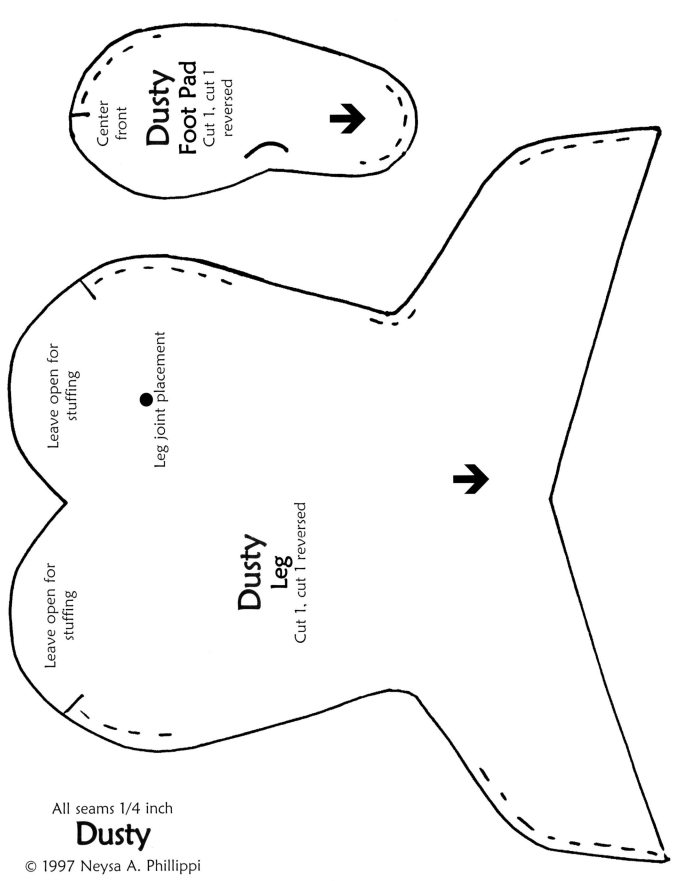

Center
front

**Dusty
Foot Pad**
Cut 1, cut 1
reversed

Leave open for
stuffing

Leg joint placement

Leave open for
stuffing

**Dusty
Leg**
Cut 1, cut 1 reversed

All seams 1/4 inch

Dusty

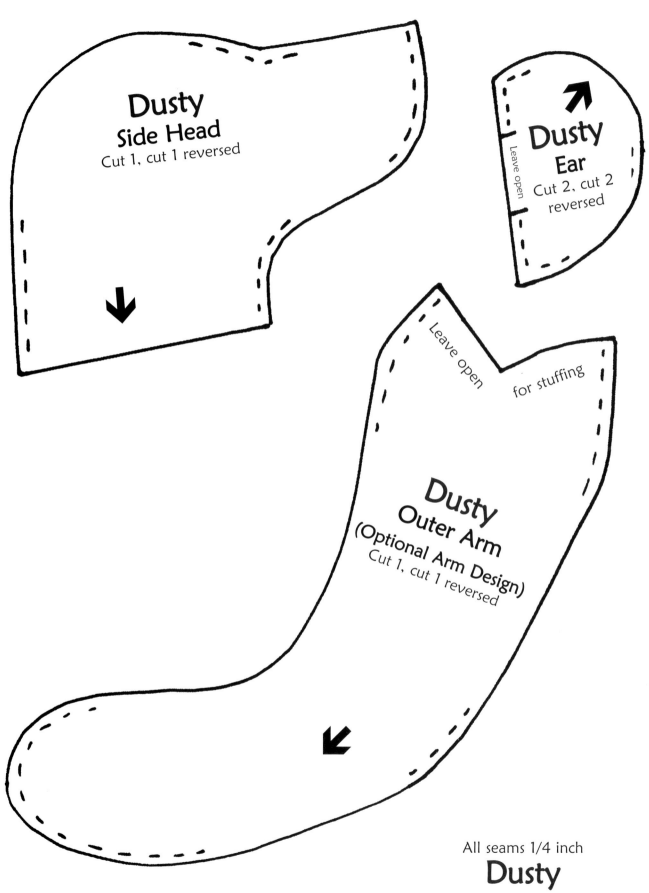

Dusty
Side Head
Cut 1, cut 1 reversed

Dusty
Ear
Cut 2, cut 2 reversed

Leave open

Leave open

for stuffing

Dusty
Outer Arm
(Optional Arm Design)
Cut 1, cut 1 reversed

All seams 1/4 inch
Dusty
© 1997 Neysa A. Phillippi

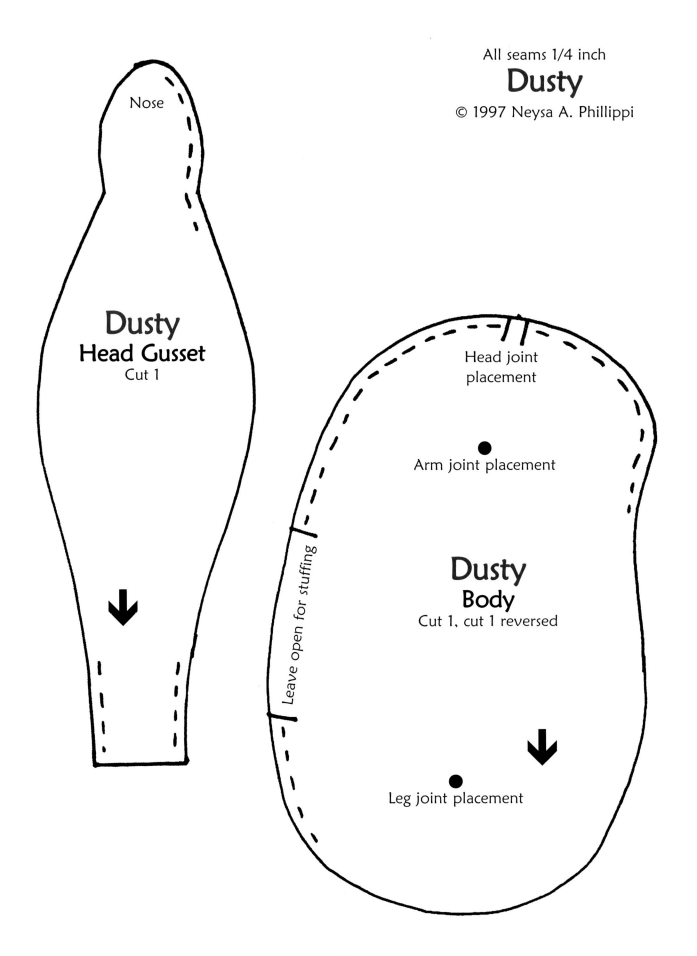

All seams 1/4 inch

Dusty
© 1997 Neysa A. Phillippi

Nose

Dusty
Head Gusset
Cut 1

Head joint placement

Arm joint placement

Dusty
Body
Cut 1, cut 1 reversed

Leave open for stuffing

Leg joint placement

All seams 1/4 inch

Dusty

© 1997 Neysa A. Phillippi

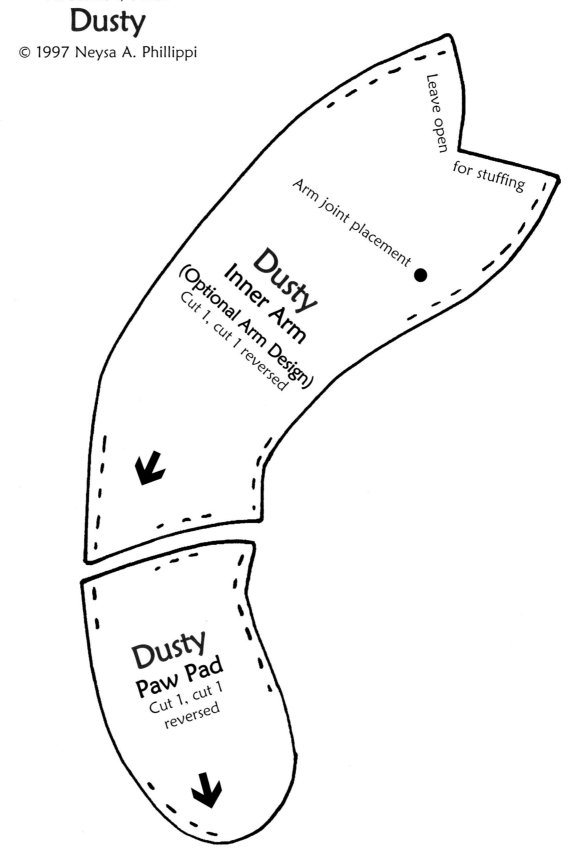

Leave open for stuffing

Arm joint placement

Dusty
Inner Arm
(Optional Arm Design)
Cut 1, cut 1 reversed

Dusty
Paw Pad
Cut 1, cut 1 reversed

Grizz

Grizz

is 17" tall (roughly 43 cm).

MATERIALS

- 1/2 yard (36" x 30") mohair, your choice style, color and length
- 6" square for contrasting Side Head Muzzle - optional
- 9" square of velour upholstery fabric, felt, ultra suede or other fabric for paw pads
- One pair 8 mm glass or plastic eyes
- 5– 45 mm joints
- Yarn for nose and mouth
- Sewing machine thread for seams to match mohair color (If you are stuffing with pellets, I recommend you sew all seams twice.)
- Nylon upholstery thread for attaching eyes and closing seams (this is what I use)
- Stuffing and plastic pellets

*** **Side Head Muzzle** may be in a contrasting color or in a different fur pile.

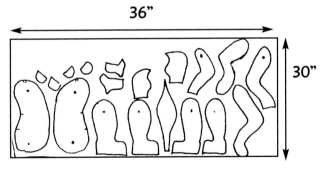

1/2 yard (36" x 30")

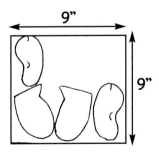

9-inch square for paw pads and foot pads

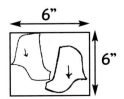

6-inch square needed if using contrasting color or different pile fur for Side Head Muzzle.
***As pictured

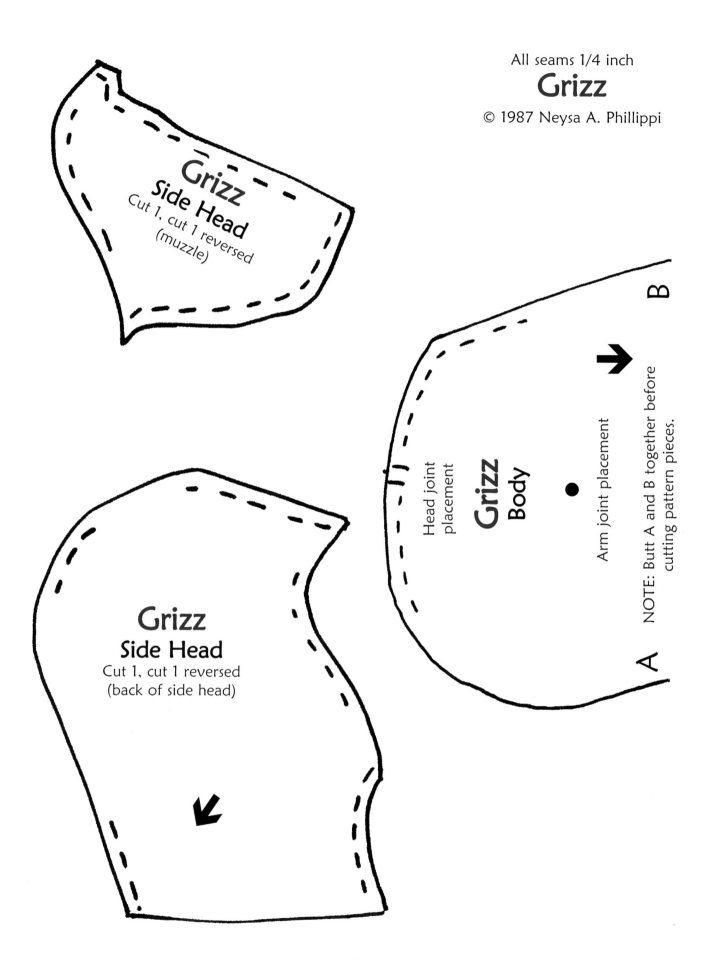

All seams 1/4 inch
Grizz
© 1987 Neysa A. Phillippi

Grizz
Side Head
Cut 1, cut 1 reversed
(muzzle)

Grizz
Side Head
Cut 1, cut 1 reversed
(back of side head)

B

Head joint placement

Grizz
Body

Arm joint placement

A NOTE: Butt A and B together before cutting pattern pieces.

82

All seams 1/4 inch

Grizz

© 1987 Neysa A. Phillippi

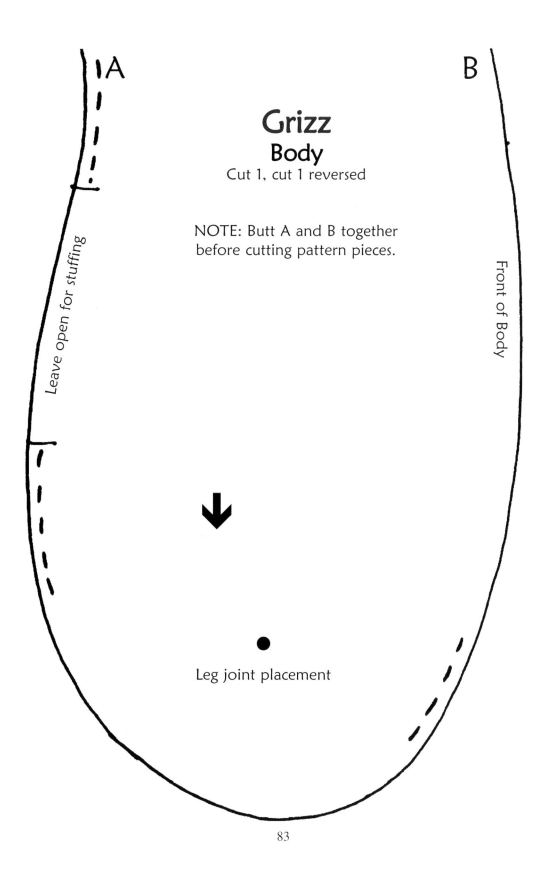

A

B

Grizz
Body
Cut 1, cut 1 reversed

NOTE: Butt A and B together
before cutting pattern pieces.

Leave open for stuffing

Front of Body

Leg joint placement

All seams 1/4 inch

Grizz

© 1987 Neysa A. Phillippi

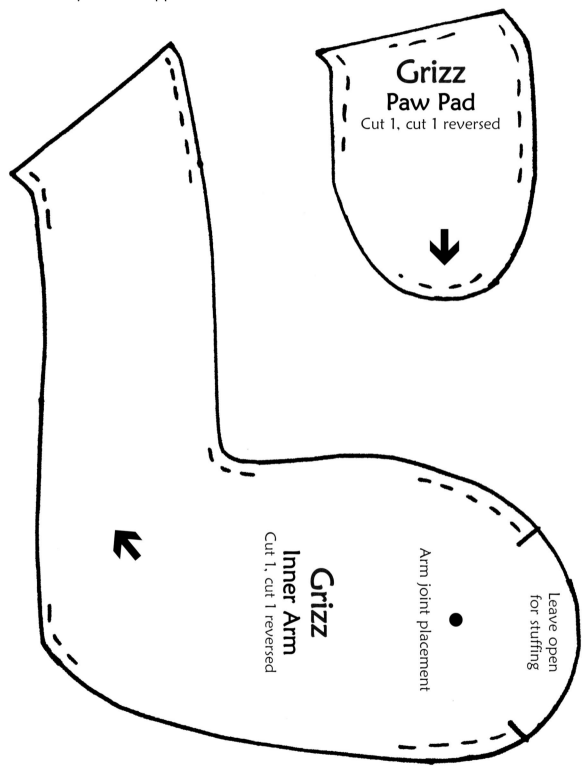

Grizz
Paw Pad
Cut 1, cut 1 reversed

Grizz
Inner Arm
Cut 1, cut 1 reversed

Arm joint placement

Leave open
for stuffing

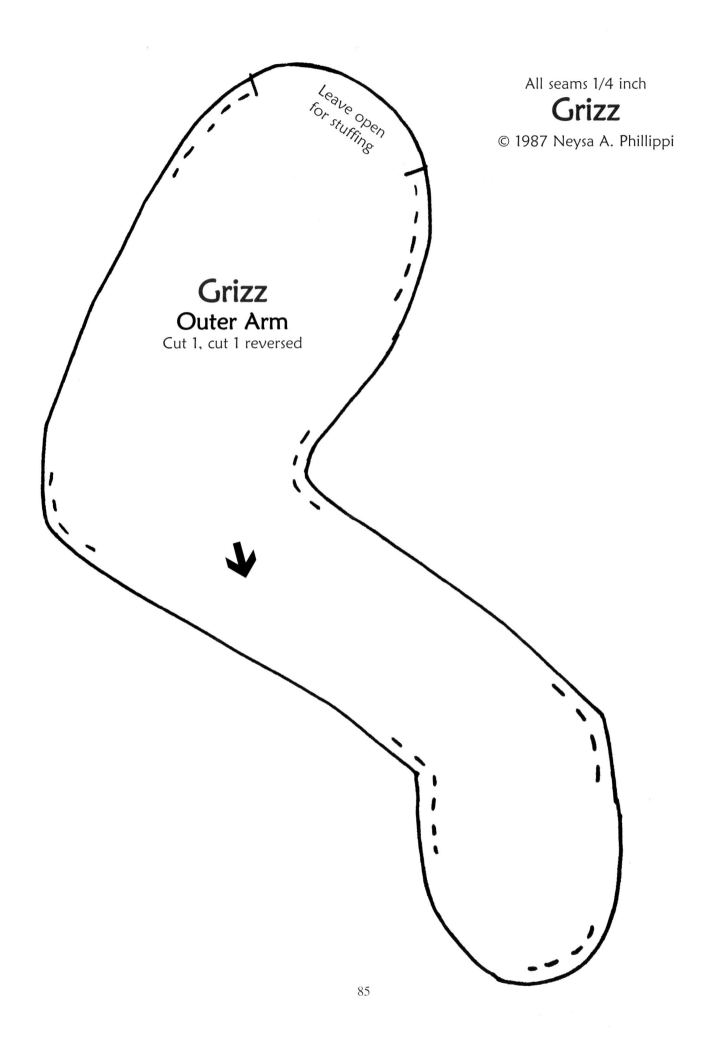

All seams 1/4 inch

Grizz

© 1987 Neysa A. Phillippi

Leave open for stuffing

Grizz
Outer Arm
Cut 1, cut 1 reversed

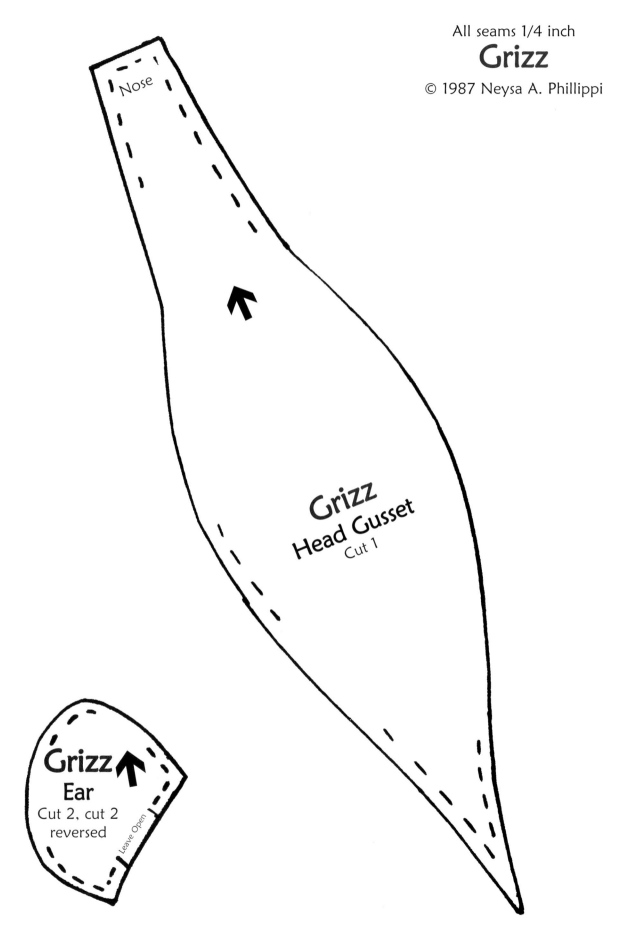

All seams 1/4 inch

Grizz
© 1987 Neysa A. Phillippi

Nose

Grizz
Head Gusset
Cut 1

Grizz
Ear
Cut 2, cut 2
reversed

Leave Open

86

All seams 1/4 inch

Grizz

© 1987 Neysa A. Phillippi

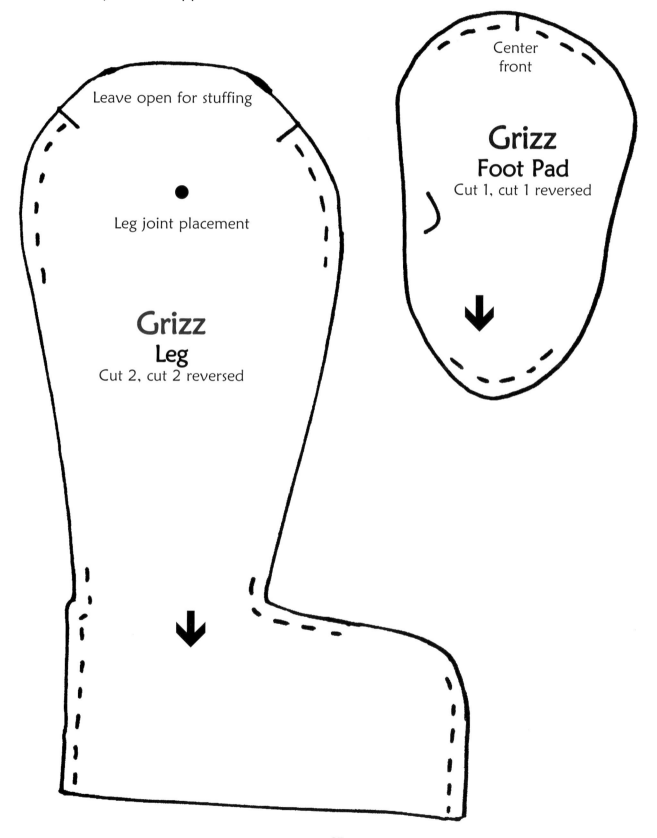

Leave open for stuffing

•

Leg joint placement

Grizz
Leg
Cut 2, cut 2 reversed

Center
front

Grizz
Foot Pad
Cut 1, cut 1 reversed

Kim Moon

Kim Moon

is 16" tall (roughly 40.5 cm) and fully jointed.

MATERIALS

- 1/4 yard (30" x 18") black mohair You may choose the style and length: for the arms, legs, upper body, ears and eye patches (optional).
- 1/8 yard (12" square) white mohair for the head and lower body
- 9" square of velour upholstery fabric, felt, ultra suede or other fabric for paw pads
- One pair 9 mm glass or plastic eyes

- 5 sets – 30 mm joints for head, arms and for the legs
- Yarn for nose and mouth
- Sewing machine thread for seams to match mohair color (If you are stuffing with pellets, I recommend you sew all seams twice.)
- Nylon upholstery thread for attaching eyes and closing seams (this is what I use)
- Stuffing and plastic pellets

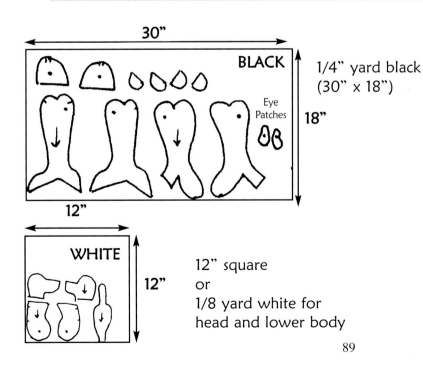

1/4" yard black (30" x 18")

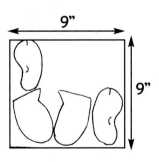

9-inch square for paw pads and foot pads

12" square
or
1/8 yard white for head and lower body

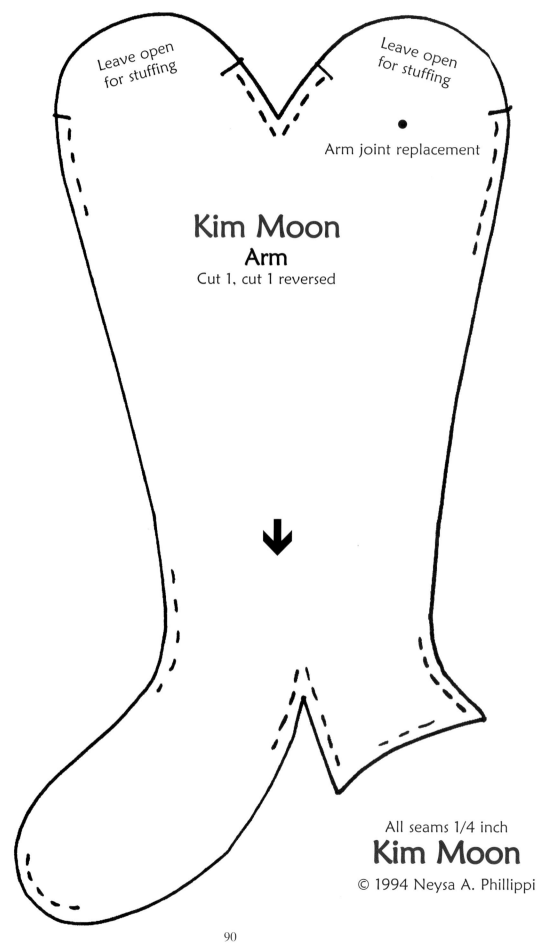

Leave open
for stuffing

Leave open
for stuffing

Arm joint replacement

Kim Moon
Arm
Cut 1, cut 1 reversed

All seams 1/4 inch
Kim Moon
© 1994 Neysa A. Phillippi

90

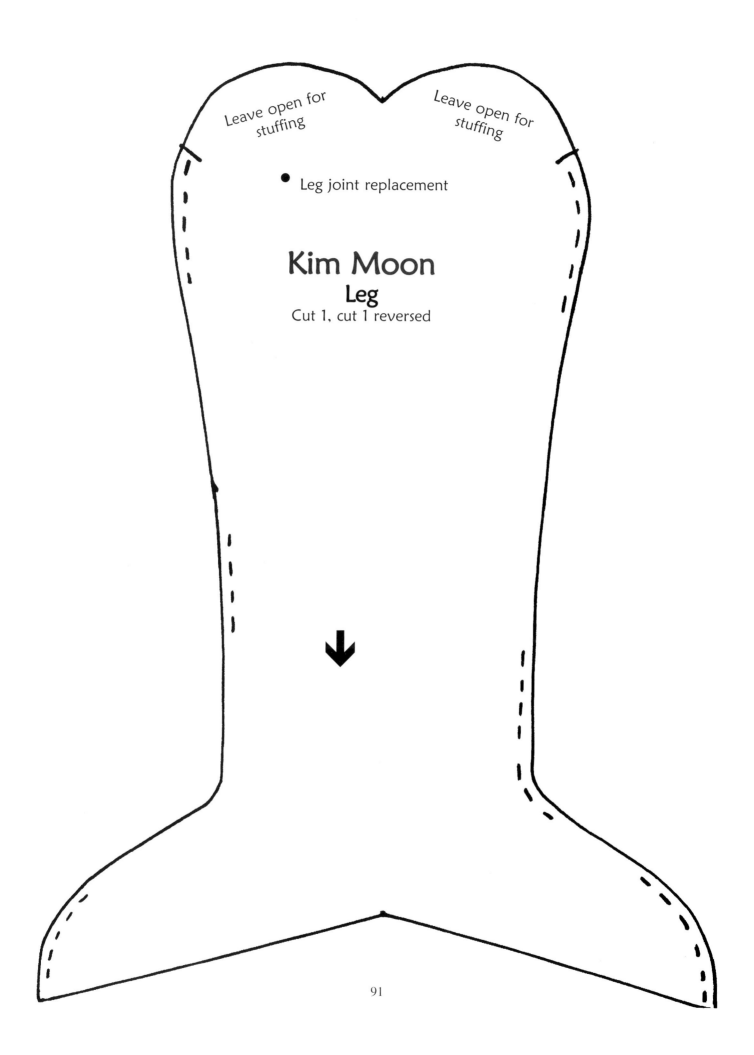

Leave open for stuffing

Leave open for stuffing

• Leg joint replacement

Kim Moon
Leg
Cut 1, cut 1 reversed

Leave open for stuffing

Leave open for stuffing

Kim Moon
Side Head
Cut 1, cut 1 reversed

Kim Moon
Paw Pad
Cut 1, cut 1
reversed

Kim Moon
Ear
Cut 2, cut 2 reversed

Leave open

Kim Moon
Eye Patch
with eye hole
Cut 1, cut 1
reversed

Center
front

Kim Moon
Foot Pad
Cut 1, cut 1
reversed

All seams 1/4 inch

Kim Moon

© 1994 Neysa A. Phillippi

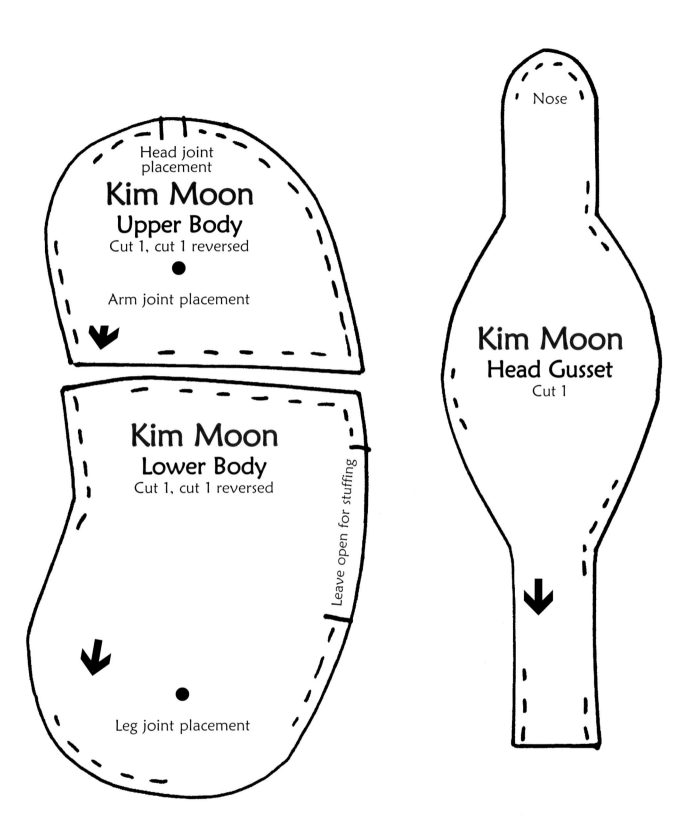

Head joint placement

Kim Moon
Upper Body
Cut 1, cut 1 reversed

Arm joint placement

Kim Moon
Lower Body
Cut 1, cut 1 reversed

Leave open for stuffing

Leg joint placement

Nose

Kim Moon
Head Gusset
Cut 1

All seams 1/4 inch
Kim Moon
© 1994 Neysa A. Phillippi

Klondike

Klondike

is 19" tall (roughly 48 cm)
and designed to lie down.

MATERIALS

- 1/2 yard (30" x 36") OR
  (18" x 58") mohair, your choice
  style, color and length.
- 9" square of velour upholstery
  fabric, felt, ultra suede or other
  fabric for paw pads
- One pair 9 mm glass or plastic eyes
- 5 sets – 35 mm joints
- Yarn for nose and mouth

- Sewing machine thread for seams to
  match mohair color (If you are
  stuffing with pellets, I recommend
  you sew all seams twice.)
- Nylon upholstery thread for
  attaching eyes and closing seams
  (this is what I use)
- Stuffing and plastic pellets

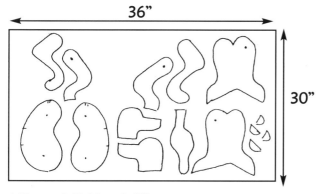

1/2 yard (30" x 36")
or
(18" x 58")

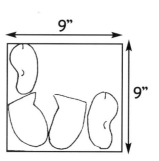

9-inch square for paw pads
and foot pads

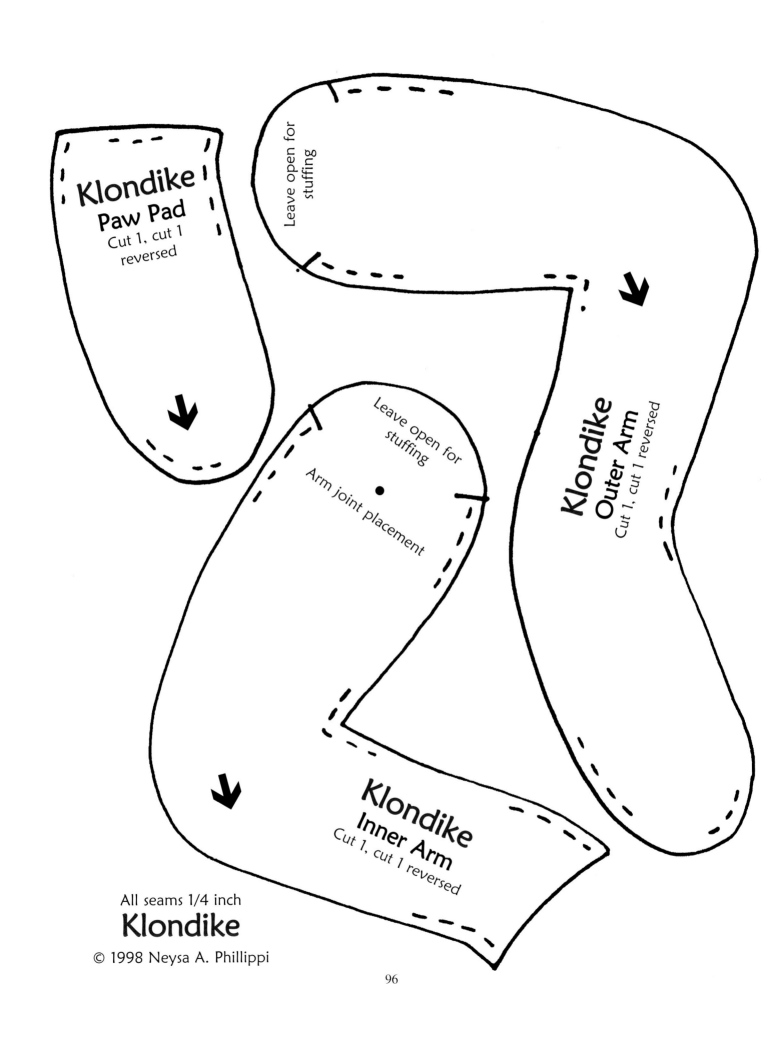

Klondike
Paw Pad
Cut 1, cut 1
reversed

Leave open for
stuffing

Klondike
Outer Arm
Cut 1, cut 1 reversed

Leave open for
stuffing

Arm joint placement

Klondike
Inner Arm
Cut 1, cut 1 reversed

All seams 1/4 inch
Klondike
© 1998 Neysa A. Phillippi

96

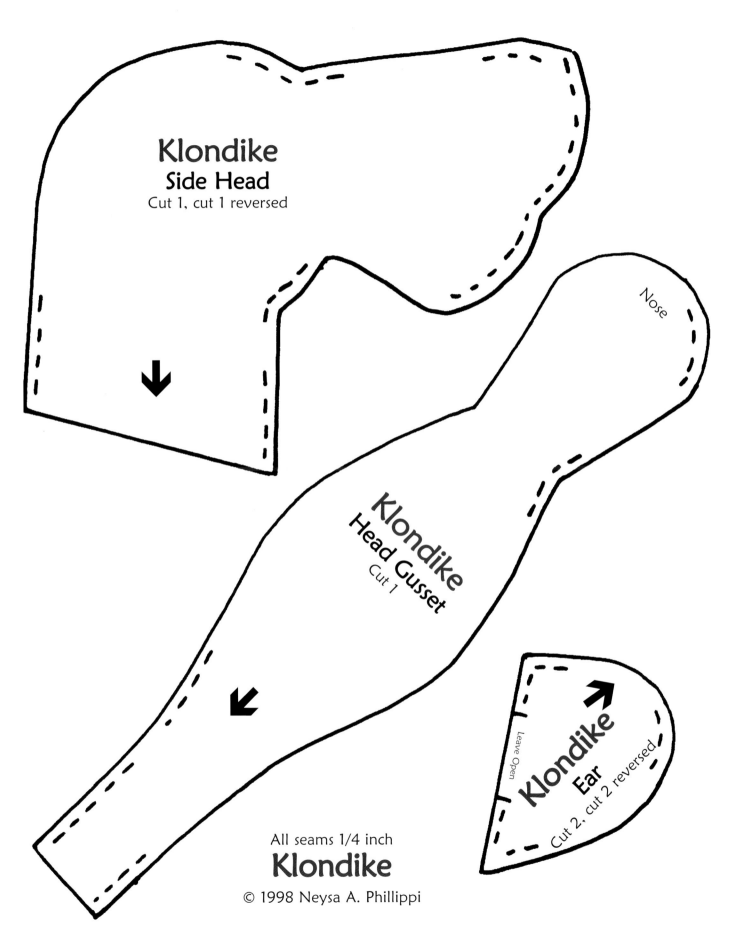

Klondike
Side Head
Cut 1, cut 1 reversed

Nose

Klondike
Head Gusset
Cut 1

Leave Open

Klondike
Ear
Cut 2, cut 2 reversed

All seams 1/4 inch

Klondike

© 1998 Neysa A. Phillippi

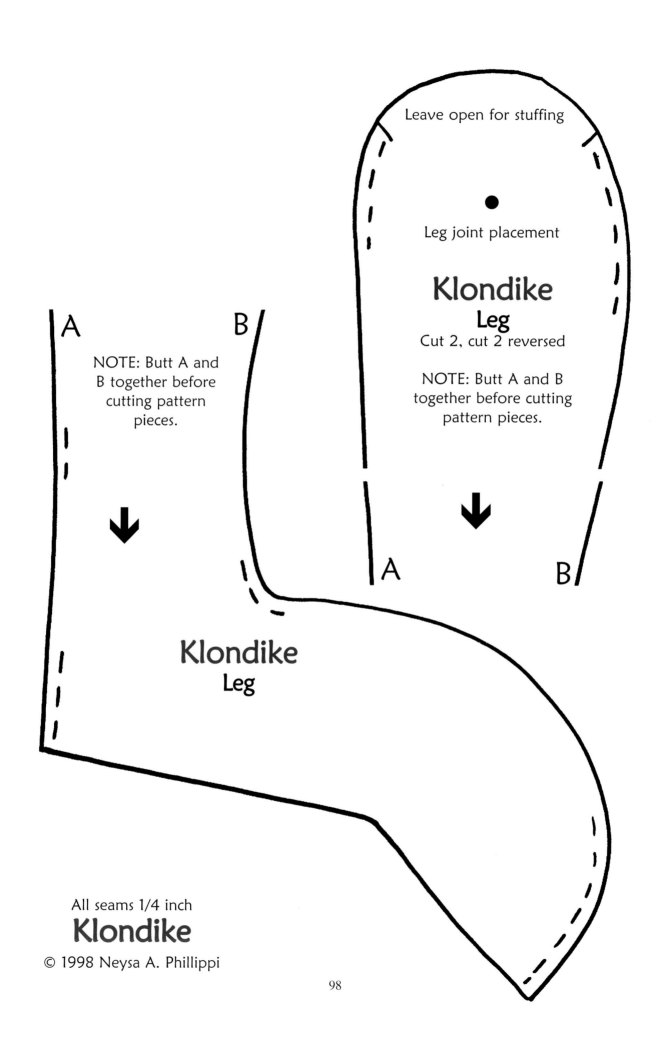

Leave open for stuffing

Leg joint placement

Klondike
Leg
Cut 2, cut 2 reversed

NOTE: Butt A and B together before cutting pattern pieces.

A

B

NOTE: Butt A and B together before cutting pattern pieces.

A

B

Klondike
Leg

All seams 1/4 inch
Klondike
© 1998 Neysa A. Phillippi

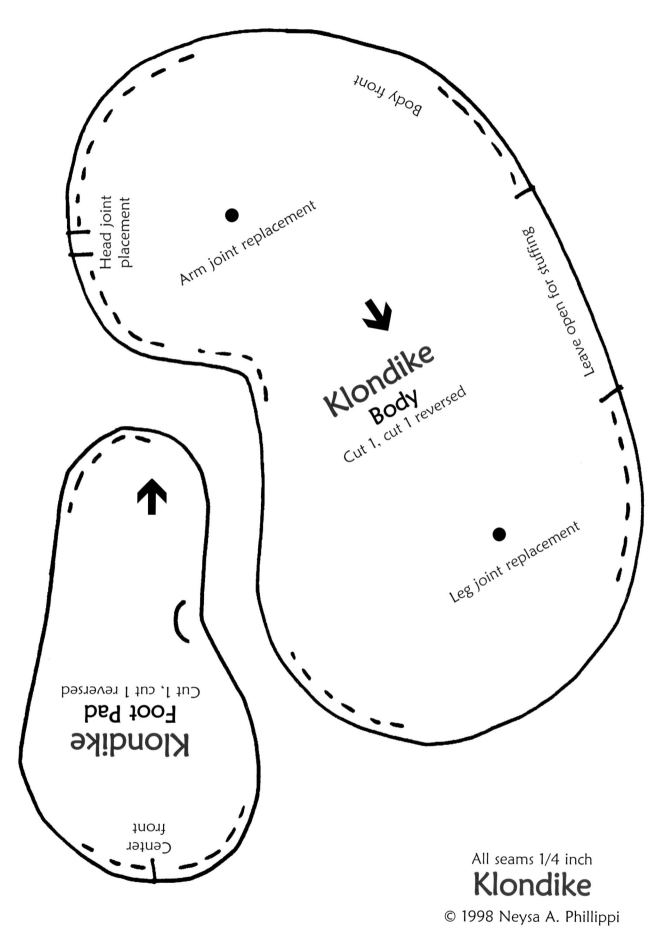

Body front

Head joint placement

Arm joint replacement

Klondike
Body
Cut 1, cut 1 reversed

Leave open for stuffing

Leg joint replacement

Klondike
Foot Pad
Cut 1, cut 1 reversed

Center front

All seams 1/4 inch
Klondike
© 1998 Neysa A. Phillippi

99

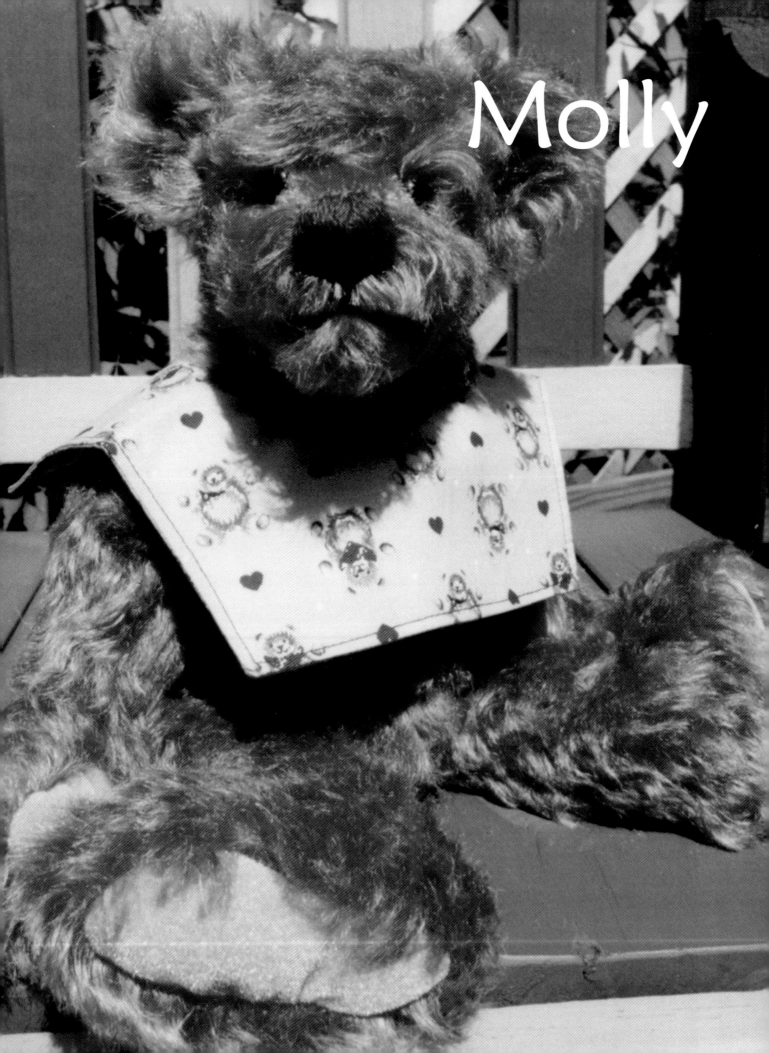

Molly

Molly

is 13" tall (roughly 33 cm).

MATERIALS

- 1/4 yard (30" x 18") or (9" x 58") mohair. You may choose the style, color and length
- 9" square of velour upholstery fabric, felt, ultra suede or other fabric for paw pads
- One pair 9 mm glass or plastic eyes
- 5 sets – 35 mm joints
- Yarn for nose and mouth

- Sewing machine thread for seams to match mohair color (If you are stuffing with pellets, I recommend you sew all seams twice.)
- Nylon upholstery thread for attaching eyes and closing seams (this is what I use)
- Stuffing and plastic pellets

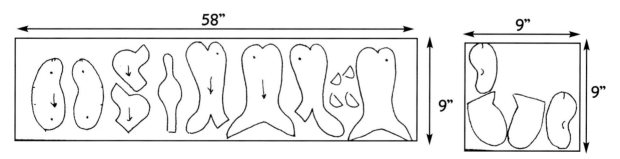

1/4 yard (58" x 9")
or
(30" x 18")

9-inch square for paw pads and foot pads

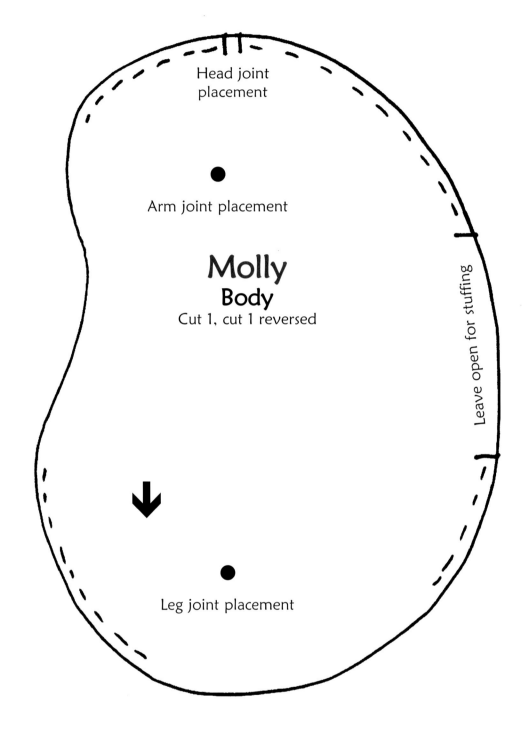

Head joint
placement

Arm joint placement

Molly
Body
Cut 1, cut 1 reversed

Leave open for stuffing

Leg joint placement

All seams 1/4 inch
Molly
© 1993 Neysa A. Phillippi

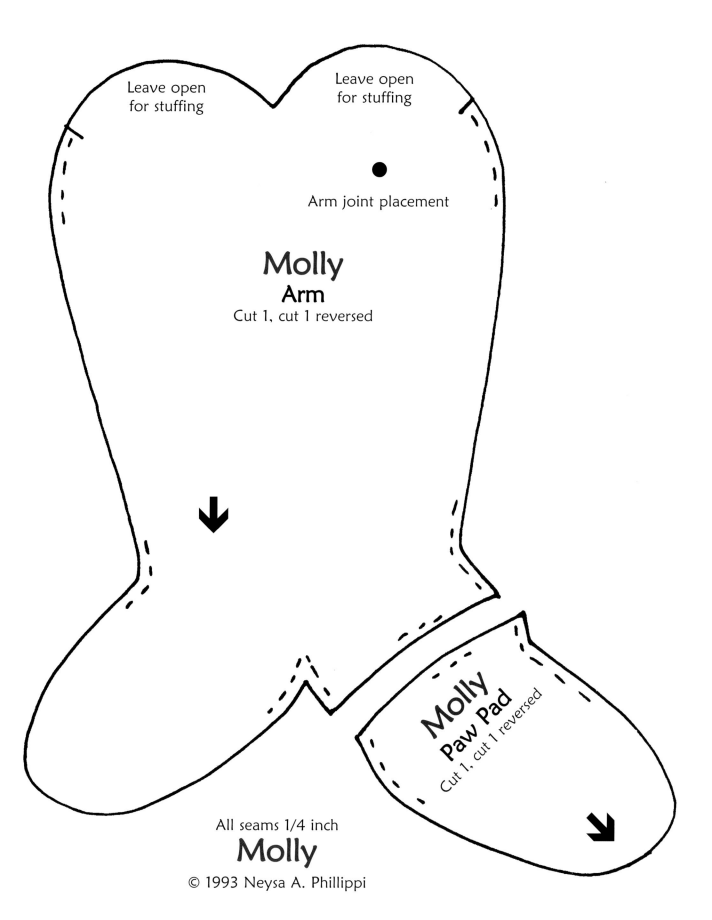

Leave open
for stuffing

Leave open
for stuffing

Arm joint placement

Molly
Arm
Cut 1, cut 1 reversed

Molly
Paw Pad
Cut 1, cut 1 reversed

All seams 1/4 inch
Molly

© 1993 Neysa A. Phillippi

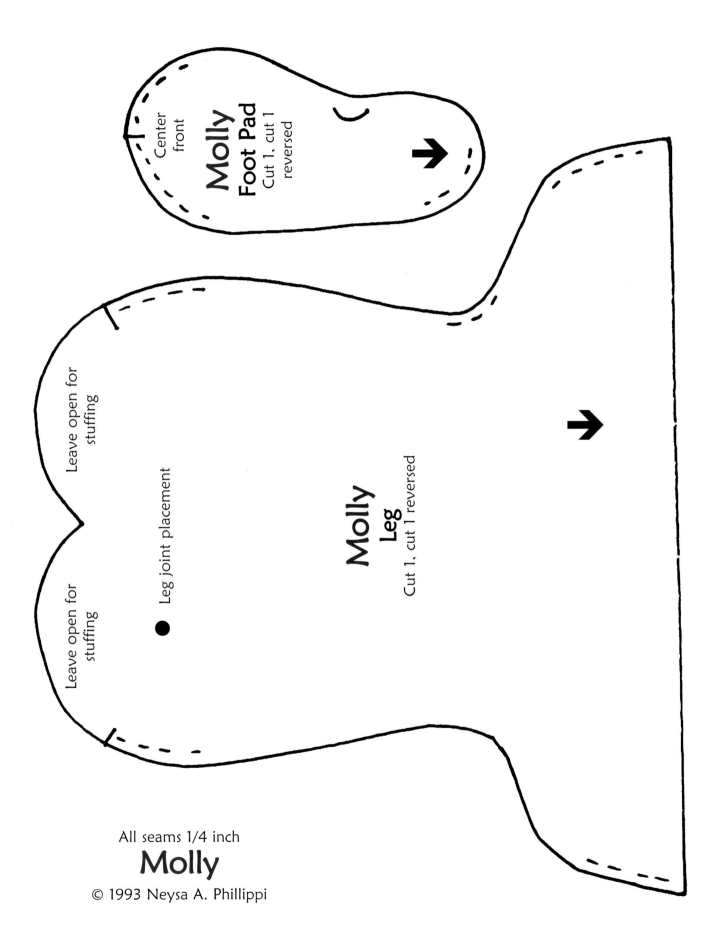

Center front

Molly
Foot Pad
Cut 1, cut 1
reversed

Leave open for stuffing

Leave open for stuffing

Leg joint placement

Molly
Leg
Cut 1, cut 1 reversed

All seams 1/4 inch

Molly

© 1993 Neysa A. Phillippi

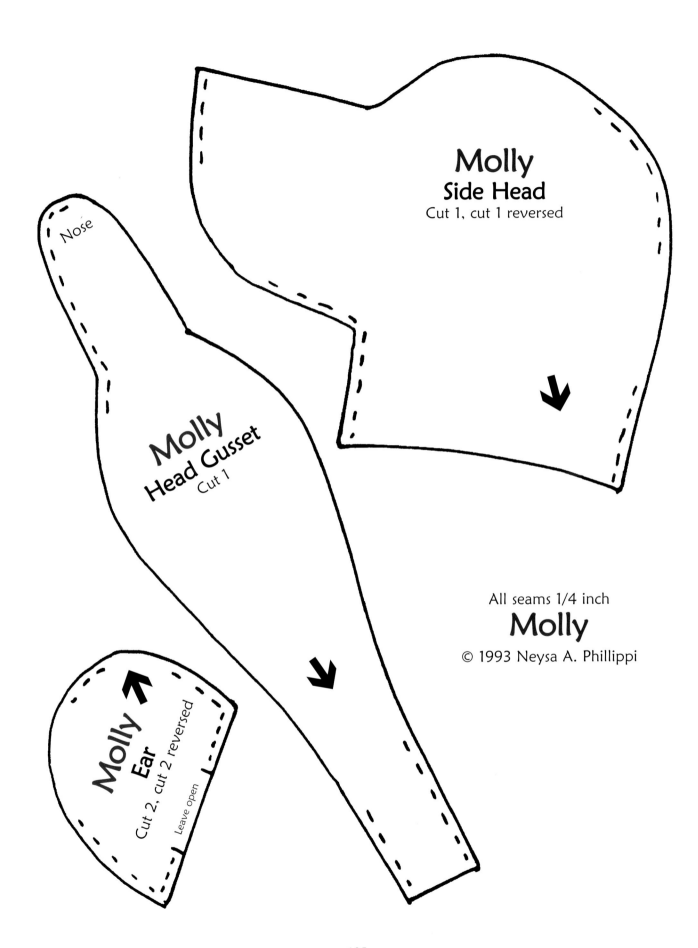

Molly
Side Head
Cut 1, cut 1 reversed

Nose

Molly
Head Gusset
Cut 1

All seams 1/4 inch
Molly
© 1993 Neysa A. Phillippi

Molly
Ear
Cut 2, cut 2 reversed

Leave open

Sidney

Sidney

is 16" (roughly 40.5 cm)
from nose to toes, and
6" (15.25cm) at the shoulders.

MATERIALS

- 1/4 yard (30" x 18") or 1/4 yard (9" x 58")mohair. You may choose the style, color and length.
- 9" square of velour upholstery fabric, felt, ultra suede or other fabric for paw pads
- One pair 8 mm glass or plastic eyes
- 5 sets – 35 mm joints
- Yarn for nose and mouth

- Sewing machine thread for seams to match mohair color (If you are stuffing with pellets, I recommend you sew all seams twice.)
- Nylon upholstery thread for attaching eyes and closing seams (this is what I use)
- Polyfil stuffing recommended

58"

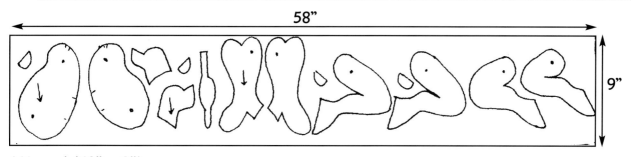

9"

1/4 yard (58" x 9")

or

1/4 yard (30" x 18")

30"

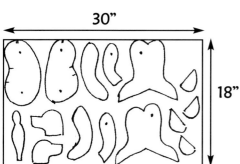

18"

9"

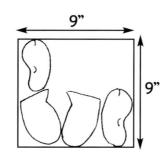

9"

9-inch square for paw pads
and foot pads

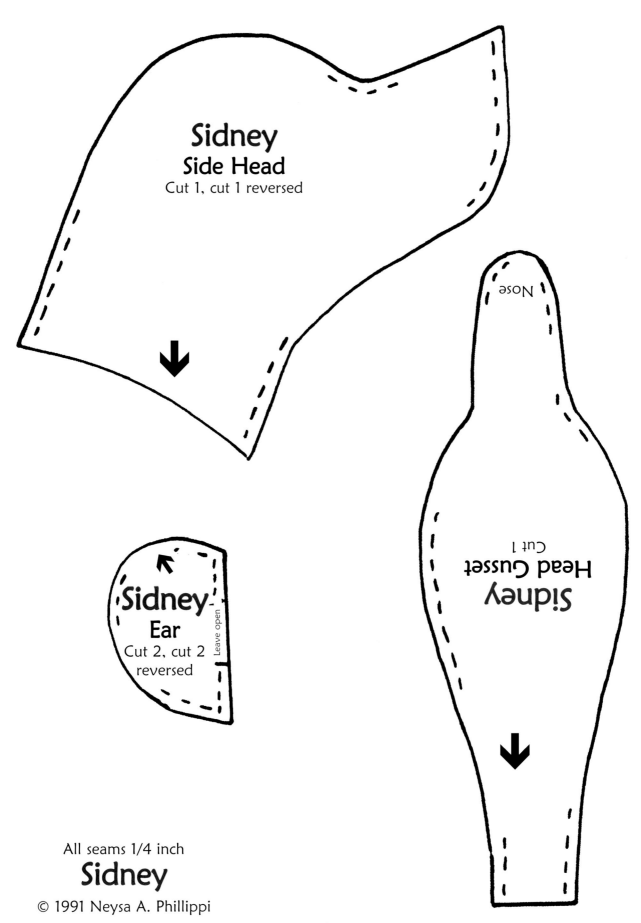

Sidney
Side Head
Cut 1, cut 1 reversed

Sidney
Ear
Cut 2, cut 2
reversed

Leave open

Nose

Sidney
Head Gusset
Cut 1

All seams 1/4 inch

Sidney

© 1991 Neysa A. Phillippi

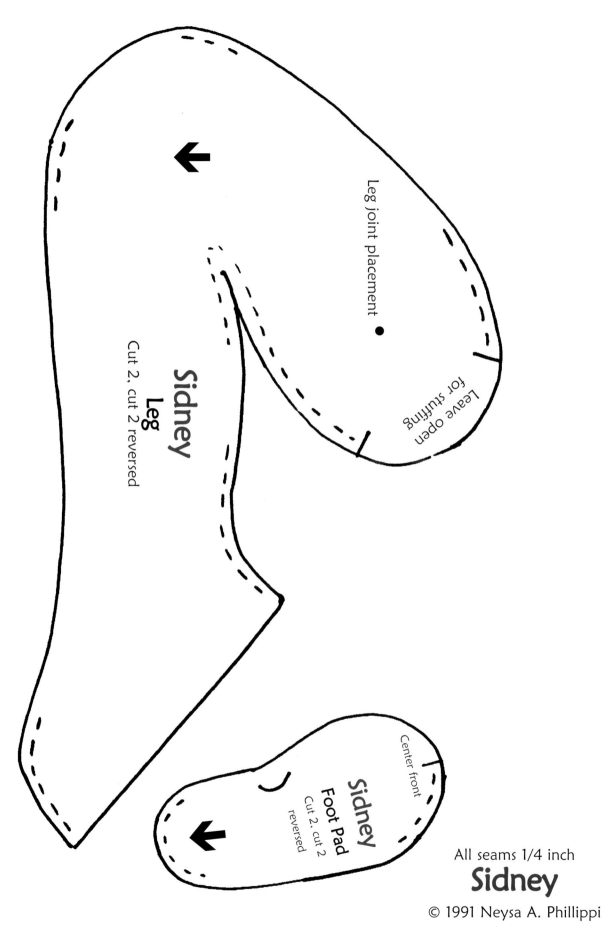

Leg joint placement ●

Leave open for stuffing

Sidney
Leg
Cut 2, cut 2 reversed

Center front

Sidney
Foot Pad
Cut 2, cut 2 reversed

All seams 1/4 inch

Sidney

© 1991 Neysa A. Phillippi

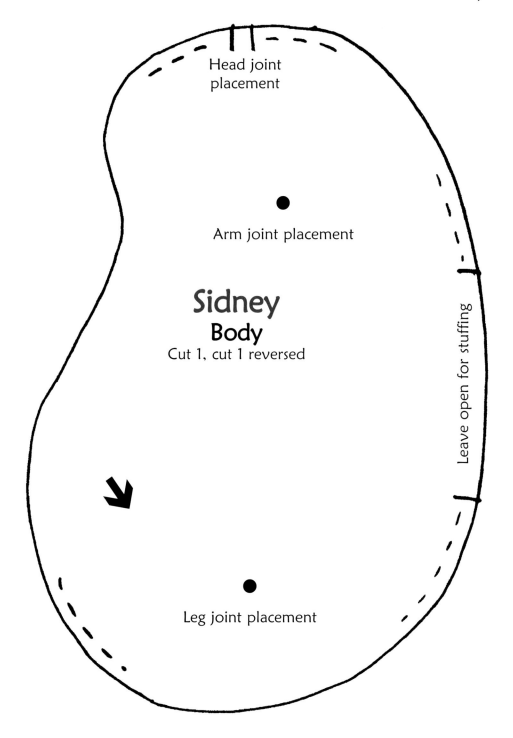

All seams 1/4 inch
Sidney
© 1991 Neysa A. Phillippi

Head joint placement

Arm joint placement

Sidney
Body
Cut 1, cut 1 reversed

Leave open for stuffing

Leg joint placement

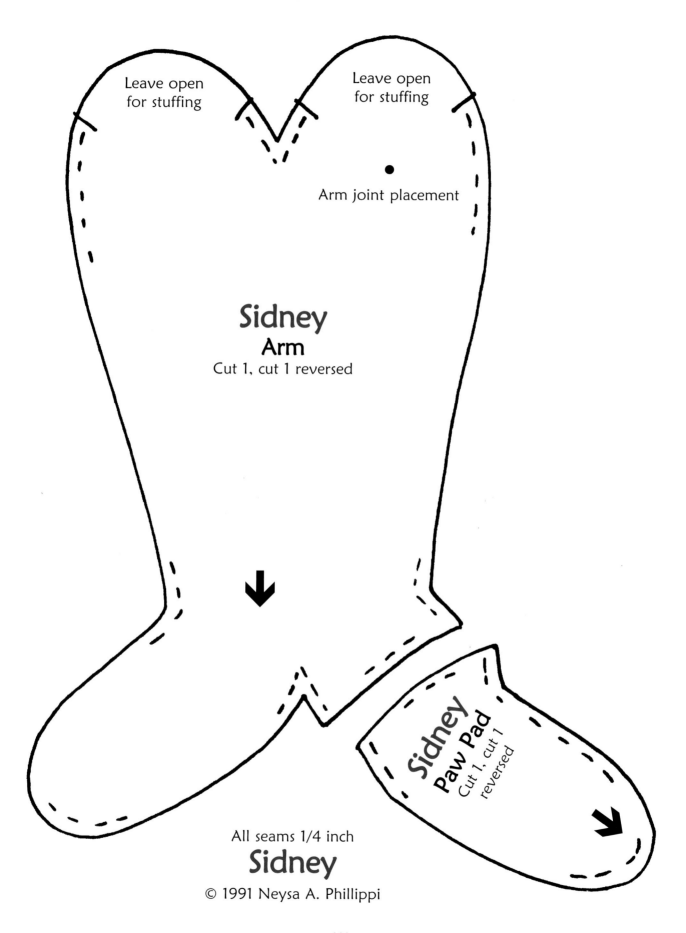

Leave open
for stuffing

Leave open
for stuffing

Arm joint placement

Sidney
Arm
Cut 1, cut 1 reversed

Sidney
Paw Pad
Cut 1, cut 1
reversed

All seams 1/4 inch
Sidney
© 1991 Neysa A. Phillippi

Taylor

Taylor

is 15" tall (roughly 38 cm) and he lies down, sits up and stands.

MATERIALS

- 1/4 yard (30" x 18") mohair, your choice style, color and length *1/4 yard measuring 9" x 58" is NOT suitable because of fabric requirements for arm/leg lengths*
- 9" square of velour upholstery fabric, felt, ultra suede or other fabric for paw pads
- One pair 9 mm glass or plastic eyes
- 5 sets – 45 mm joints

- Yarn for nose and mouth
- Sewing machine thread for seams to match mohair color (If you are stuffing with pellets, I recommend you sew all seams twice.)
- Nylon upholstery thread for attaching eyes and closing seams (this is what I use)
- Stuffing and plastic pellets

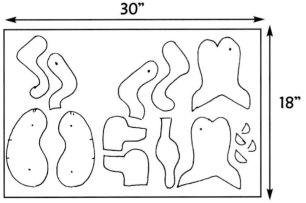

1/4 yard (18" x 30")

1/4 yard measuring 9" x 58" is NOT suitable; the arms require more length.

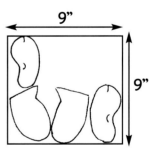

9-inch square for paw pads and foot pads

All seams 1/4 inch

Taylor

© 1995 Neysa A. Phillippi

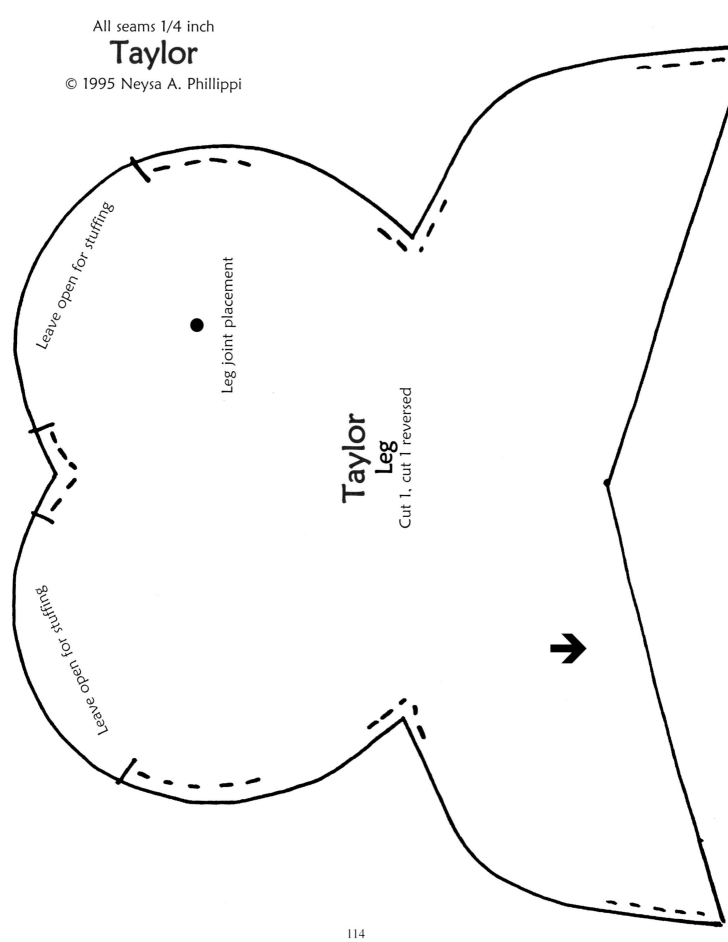

Leave open for stuffing

Leg joint placement

Leave open for stuffing

Taylor
Leg
Cut 1, cut 1 reversed

114

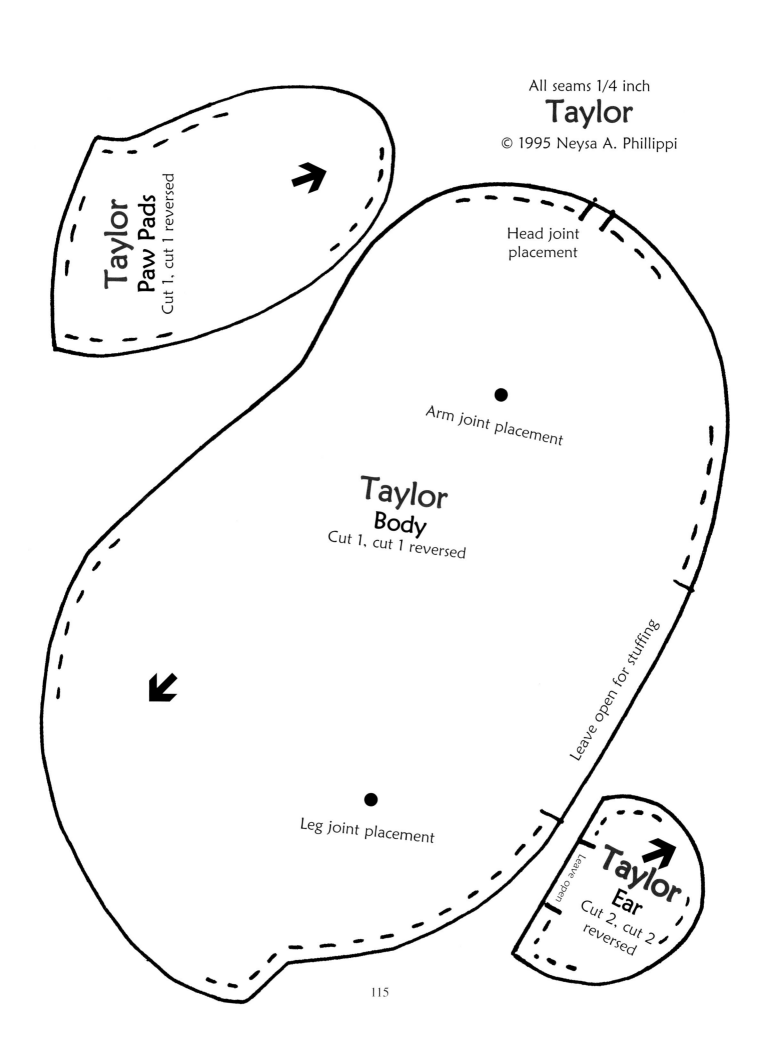

All seams 1/4 inch
Taylor
© 1995 Neysa A. Phillippi

Taylor
Paw Pads
Cut 1, cut 1 reversed

Head joint
placement

Arm joint placement

Taylor
Body
Cut 1, cut 1 reversed

Leave open for stuffing

Leg joint placement

Taylor
Ear
Cut 2, cut 2 reversed

Leave open

115

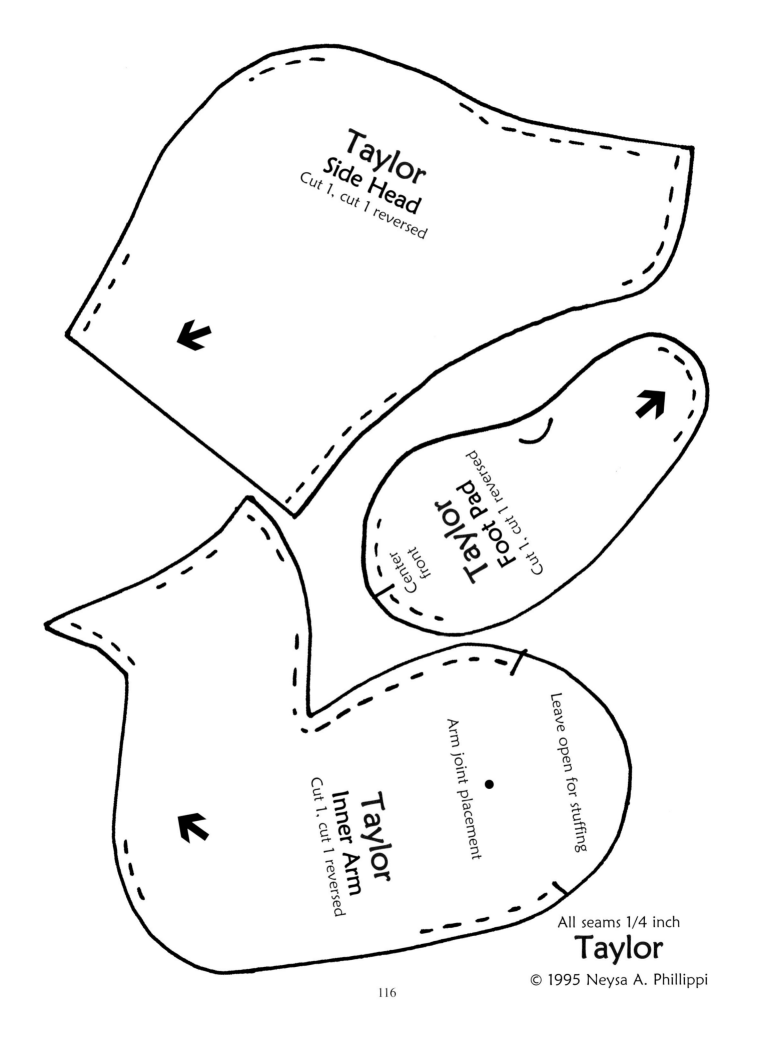

Taylor
Side Head
Cut 1, cut 1 reversed

Taylor
Foot Pad
Cut 1, cut 1 reversed

Center
front

Taylor
Inner Arm
Cut 1, cut 1 reversed

Arm joint placement

Leave open for stuffing

All seams 1/4 inch
Taylor
© 1995 Neysa A. Phillippi

116

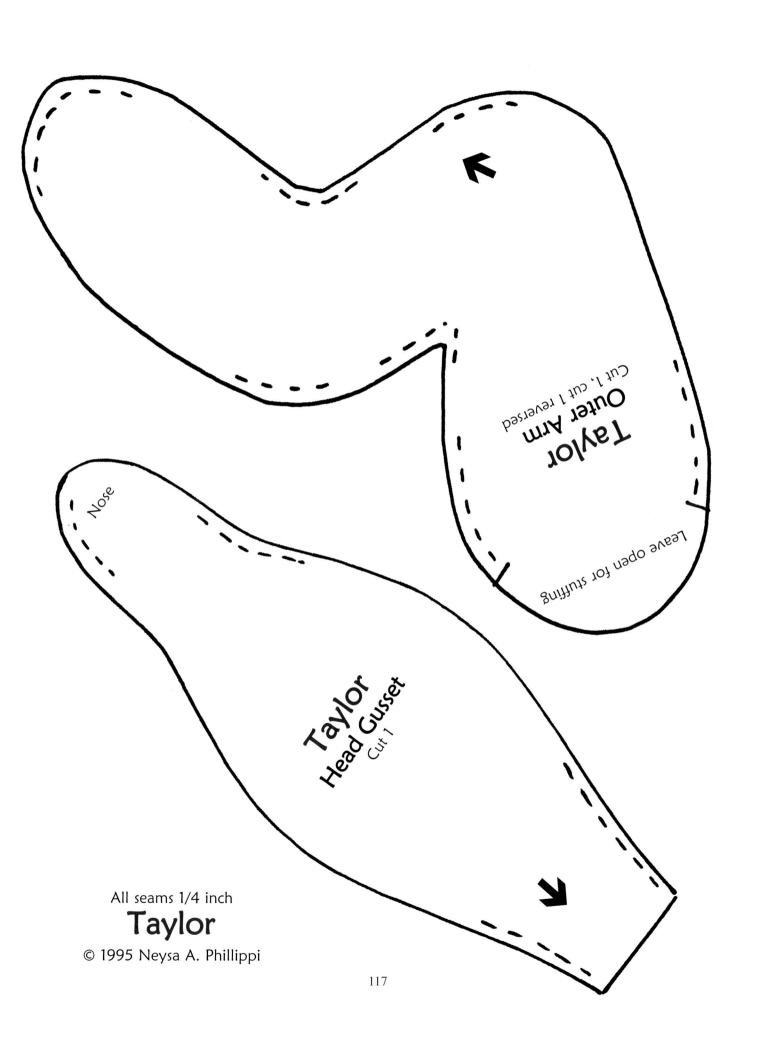

Nose

Taylor
Outer Arm
Cut 1, cut 1 reversed

Leave open for stuffing

Taylor
Head Gusset
Cut 1

All seams 1/4 inch
Taylor
© 1995 Neysa A. Phillippi

117

Vladimir

Vladimir

is 15" tall (roughly 38 cm).

MATERIALS

- 1/4 yard (30" x 18") mohair. You may choose the style, color and length
- 1/4 yard (30" x 18") plush for the coat
- 9" square of velour upholstery fabric felt, ultra suede or other fabric for paw pads
- One pair 9 mm glass or plastic eyes
- 3 sets – 35 mm joints for head and arms; 2 sets – 45 mm joints for legs
- Yarn for nose and mouth
- Sewing machine thread for seams to match mohair color (If you are stuffing with pellets, I recommend you sew all seams twice.)
- Nylon upholstery thread for attaching eyes and closing seams (this is what I use)
- Stuffing and plastic pellets
- 2 buttons for coat

*** **Read Optional Arm** on page 23; this is the arm used for Vladimir.

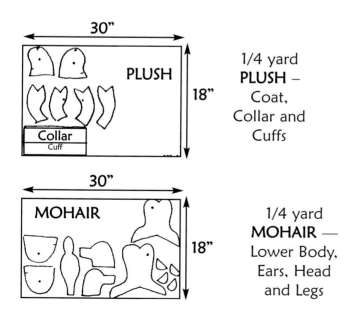

1/4 yard
PLUSH –
Coat,
Collar and
Cuffs

1/4 yard
MOHAIR —
Lower Body,
Ears, Head
and Legs

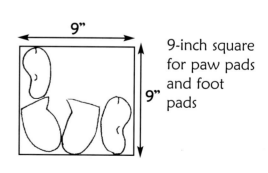

9-inch square
for paw pads
and foot
pads

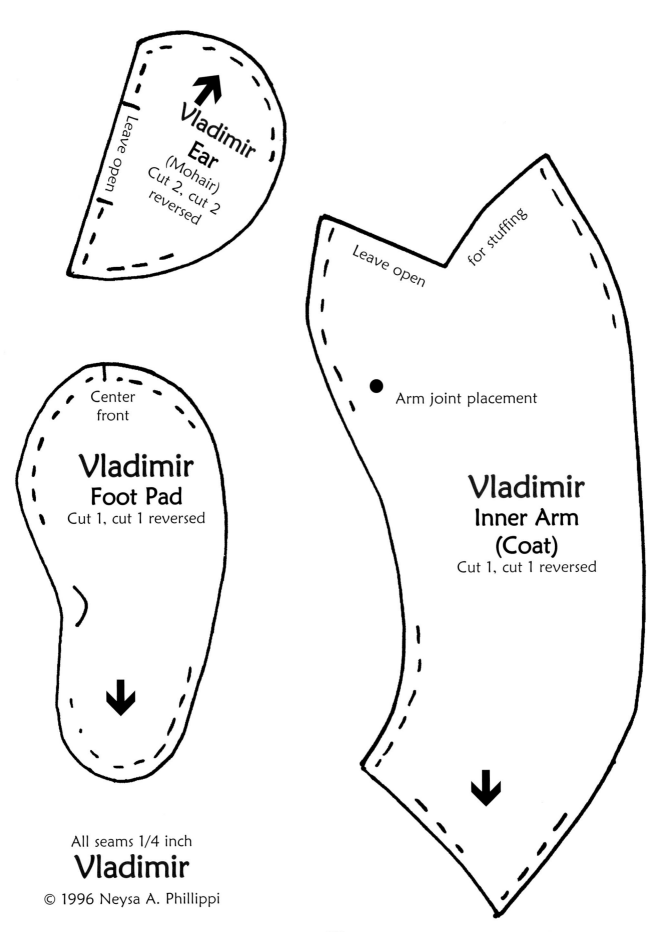

Vladimir
Ear
(Mohair)
Cut 2, cut 2 reversed

Leave open

Leave open / for stuffing

Arm joint placement

Vladimir
Inner Arm
(Coat)
Cut 1, cut 1 reversed

Center front

Vladimir
Foot Pad
Cut 1, cut 1 reversed

All seams 1/4 inch
Vladimir

© 1996 Neysa A. Phillippi

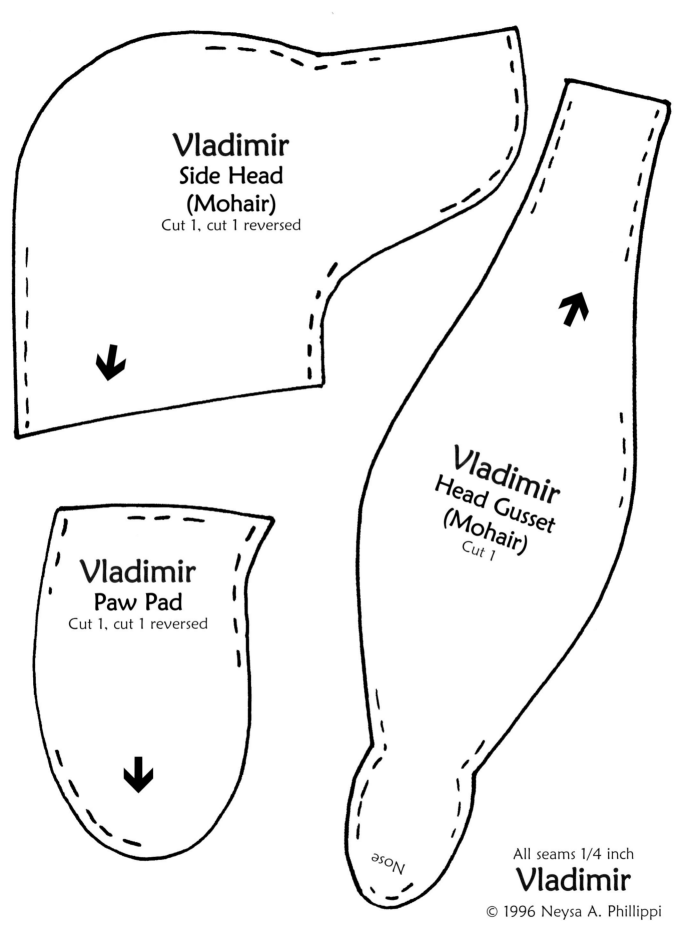

Vladimir
Side Head
(Mohair)
Cut 1, cut 1 reversed

Vladimir
Head Gusset
(Mohair)
Cut 1

Vladimir
Paw Pad
Cut 1, cut 1 reversed

Nose

All seams 1/4 inch
Vladimir
© 1996 Neysa A. Phillippi

121

All seams 1/4 inch
Vladimir
© 1996 Neysa A. Phillippi

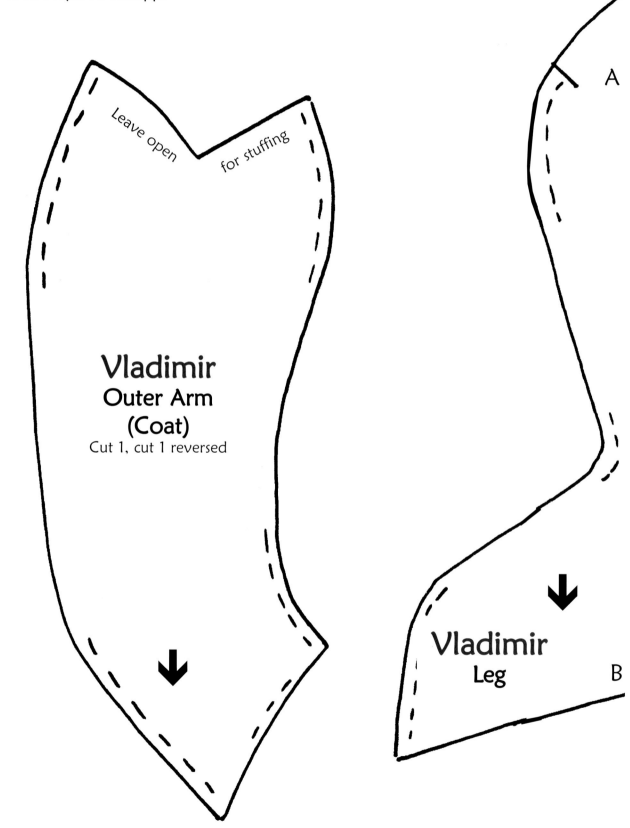

Leave open for stuffing

Vladimir
Outer Arm
(Coat)
Cut 1, cut 1 reversed

A

Vladimir
Leg

B

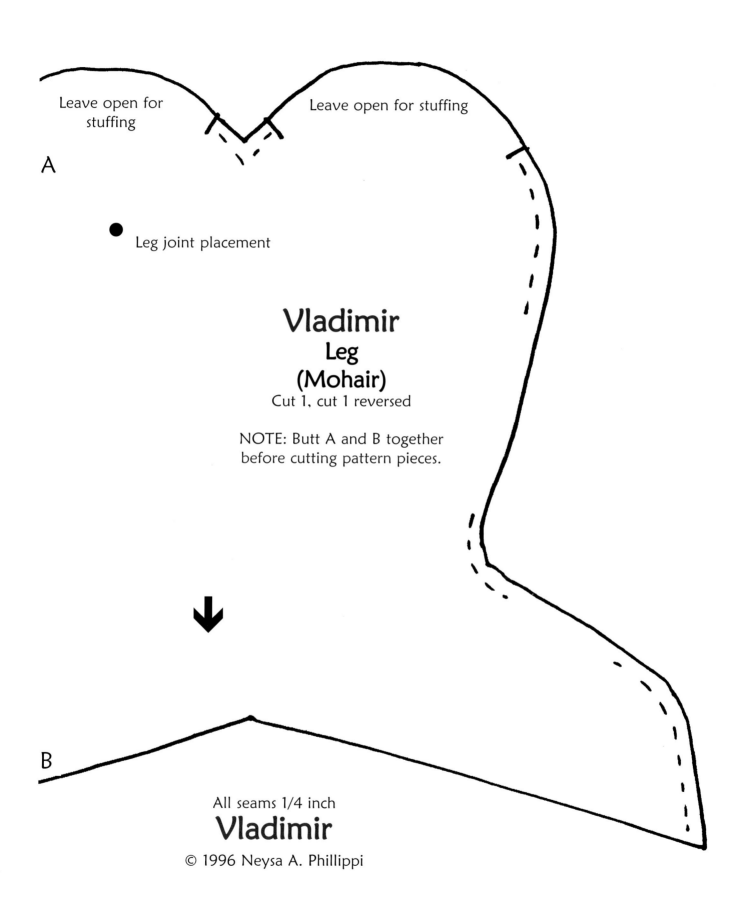

Leave open for stuffing

Leave open for stuffing

A

● Leg joint placement

Vladimir
Leg
(Mohair)
Cut 1, cut 1 reversed

NOTE: Butt A and B together before cutting pattern pieces.

B

All seams 1/4 inch
Vladimir
© 1996 Neysa A. Phillippi

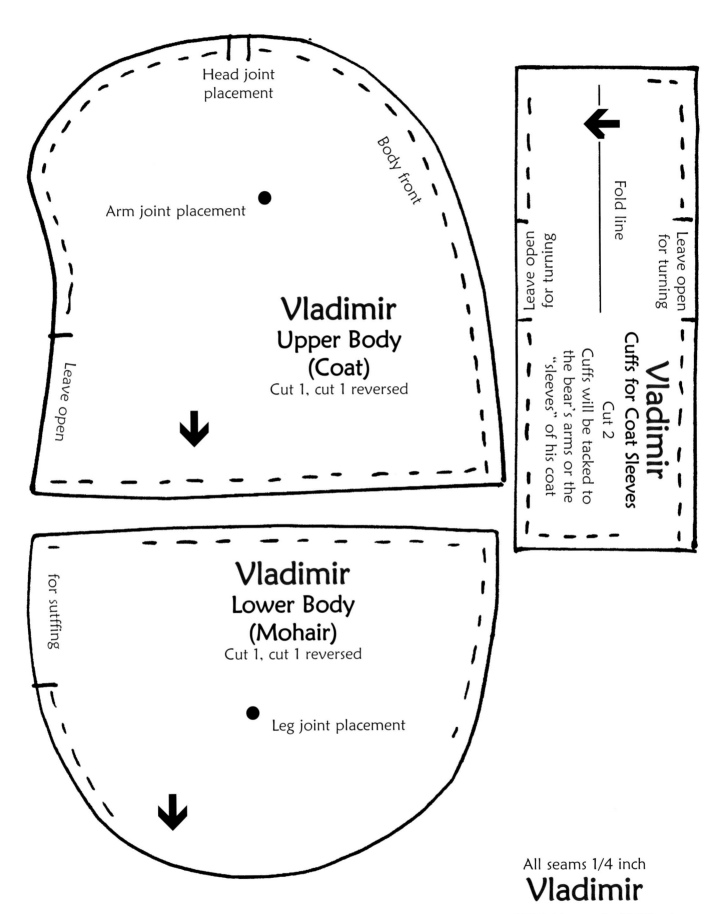

Head joint placement

Body front

Arm joint placement

Vladimir
Upper Body
(Coat)
Cut 1, cut 1 reversed

Leave open

Vladimir
Cuffs for Coat Sleeves
Cut 2
Cuffs will be tacked to the bear's arms or the "sleeves" of his coat

Fold line

Leave open for turning

Leave open for turning

Vladimir
Lower Body
(Mohair)
Cut 1, cut 1 reversed

for sutffing

Leg joint placement

All seams 1/4 inch
Vladimir

Vladimir
Collar for Coat
Cut 1

*Collar will be tacked to bear's coat (body) with a button when finished

Fold line

Leave open for turning

Leave open for turning

Wilbur

Wilbur

is 13" tall (roughly 33 cm).

MATERIALS

- 1/4 yard (30" x 18") mohair. You may choose the style, color and length.
  1/4 yard (9" x 58") is NOT suitable because of fabric requirements for arm/leg lengths
- 9" square of velour upholstery fabric, felt, ultra suede or other fabric for paw pads
- One pair 9 mm glass or plastic eyes

- 5 sets – 30 mm joints
- Yarn for nose and mouth
- Sewing machine thread for seams to match mohair color (If you are stuffing with pellets, I recommend you sew all seams twice.)
- Nylon upholstery thread for attaching eyes and closing seams (this is what I use)
- Stuffing and plastic pellets

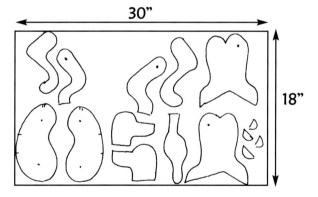

1/4 yard (30" x 18")
***1/4 yard piece of fabric measuring 9" x 54" is NOT suitable; the arms and legs require more than 9" for the arm and leg lengths.

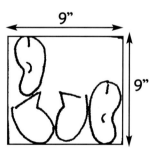

9-inch square for paw pads and foot pads

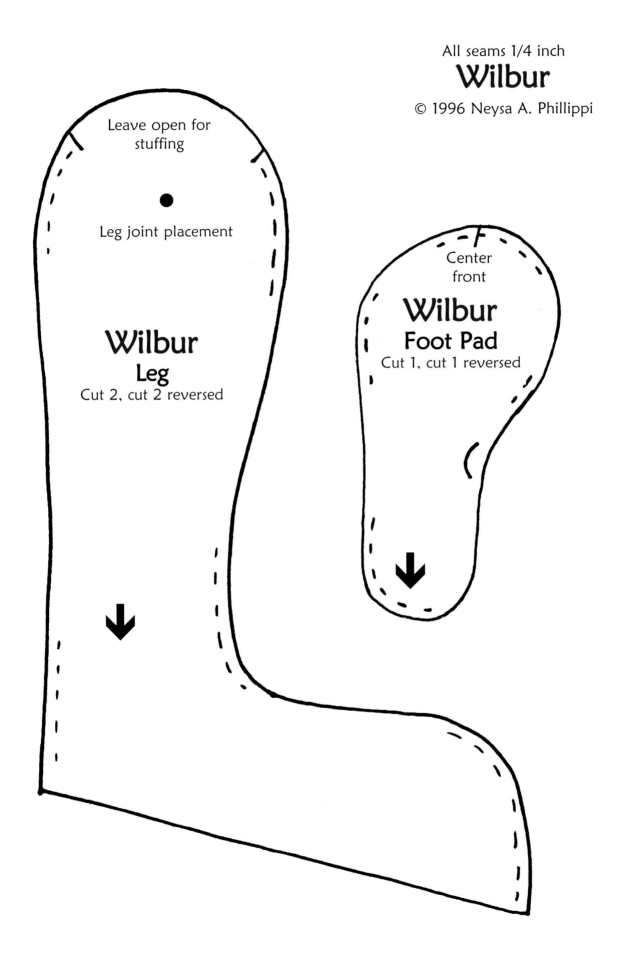

All seams 1/4 inch
Wilbur
© 1996 Neysa A. Phillippi

Leave open for stuffing

Leg joint placement

Wilbur
Leg
Cut 2, cut 2 reversed

Center front

Wilbur
Foot Pad
Cut 1, cut 1 reversed

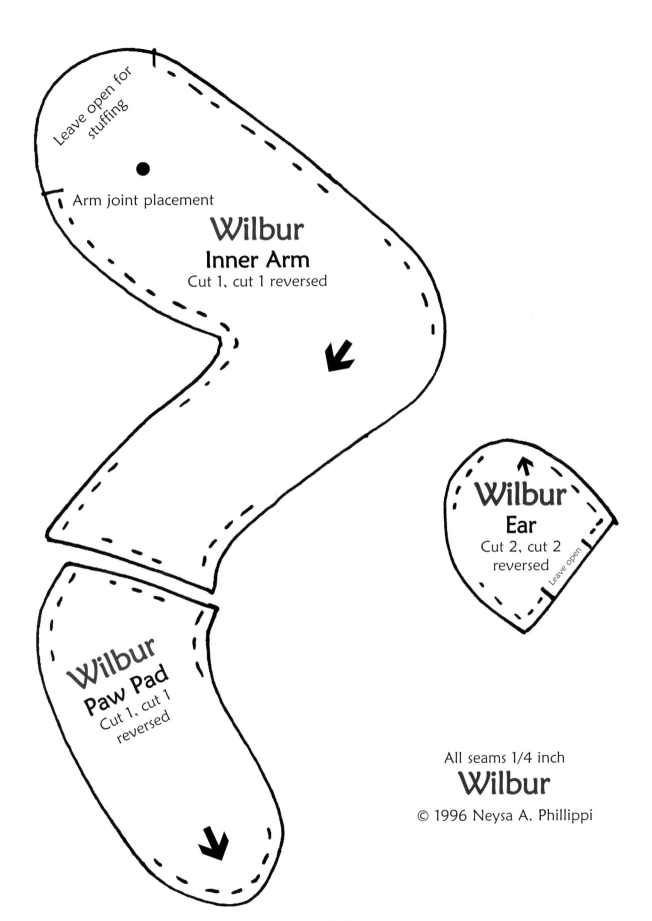

Leave open for stuffing

Arm joint placement

Wilbur
Inner Arm
Cut 1, cut 1 reversed

Wilbur
Ear
Cut 2, cut 2 reversed

Leave open

Wilbur
Paw Pad
Cut 1, cut 1 reversed

All seams 1/4 inch
Wilbur
© 1996 Neysa A. Phillippi

129

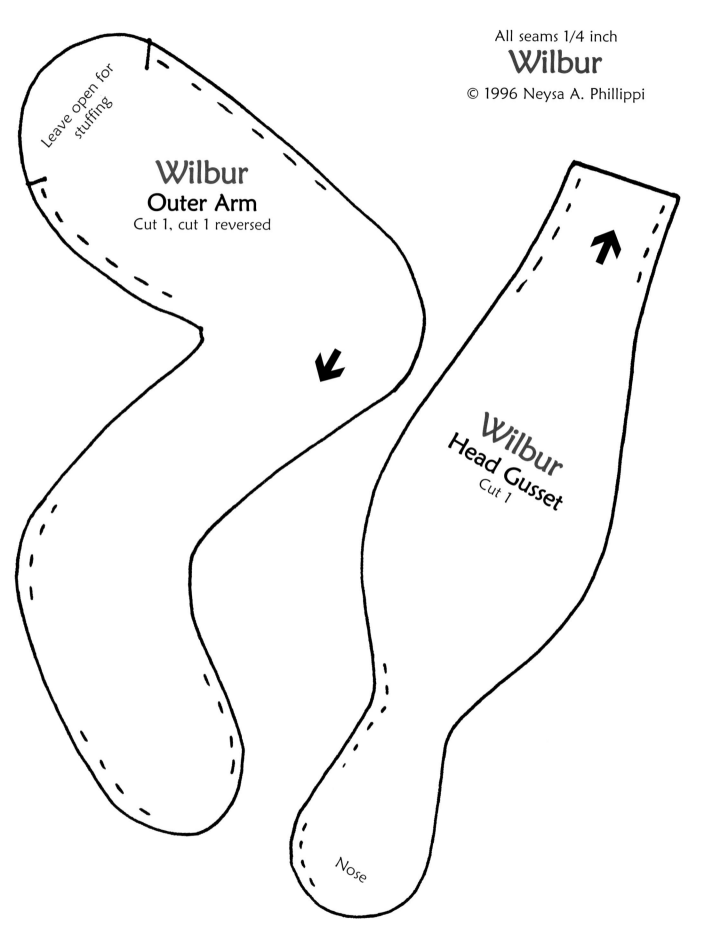

All seams 1/4 inch
Wilbur
© 1996 Neysa A. Phillippi

Leave open for stuffing

Wilbur
Outer Arm
Cut 1, cut 1 reversed

Wilbur
Head Gusset
Cut 1

Nose

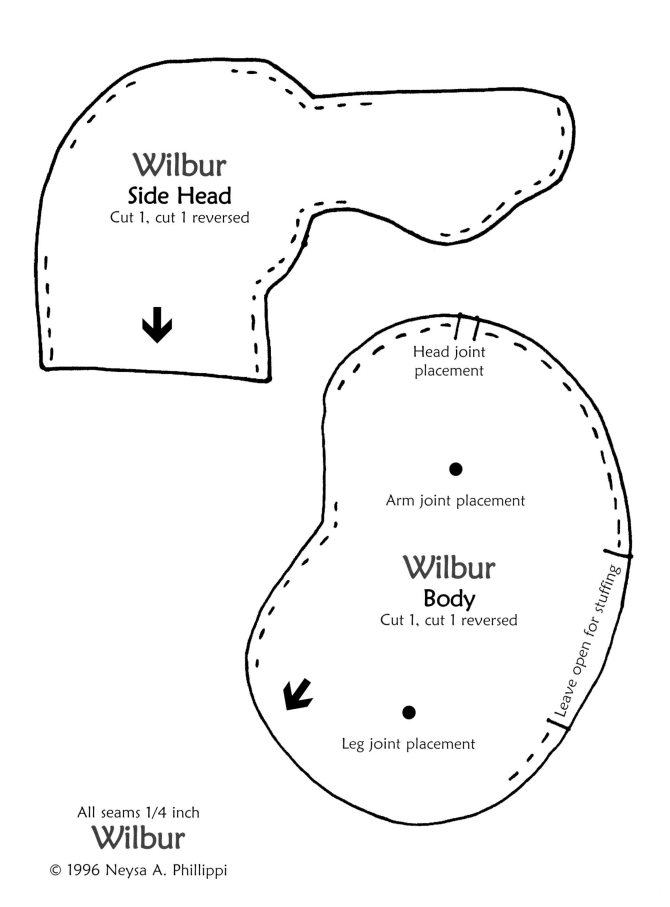

Wilbur
Side Head
Cut 1, cut 1 reversed

Head joint
placement

Arm joint placement

Wilbur
Body
Cut 1, cut 1 reversed

Leave open for stuffing

Leg joint placement

All seams 1/4 inch
Wilbur

© 1996 Neysa A. Phillippi

Winston

Winston

is 15" tall (roughly 38 cm)
and fully jointed.

MATERIALS

- 1/2 yard (36" x 30") mohair. You may choose the style, color and length.
- 9" square of velour upholstery fabric, felt, ultra suede or other fabric for paw pads
- One pair 9 mm glass or plastic eyes
- 5 sets – 45 mm joints for head, arms and legs
- Yarn for nose and mouth
- Sewing machine thread for seams to match mohair color (If you are stuffing with pellets, I recommend you sew all seams twice.)
- Nylon upholstery thread for attaching eyes and closing seams (this is what I use)
- Stuffing and plastic pellets
- *** Winston has two different styles of arms, the traditional and my **optional arm** on page 25. Be sure you follow directions on pattern pieces for the exact layout of these pieces. You have two different outer arms, inner arms and paw pads.

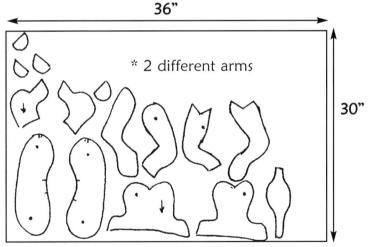

36"

* 2 different arms

30"

1/2 yard (36" x 30")

Remember you have two different arms.
Follow directions on pattern pieces.

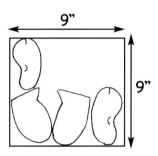

9"

9"

9-inch square for paw pads
and foot pads

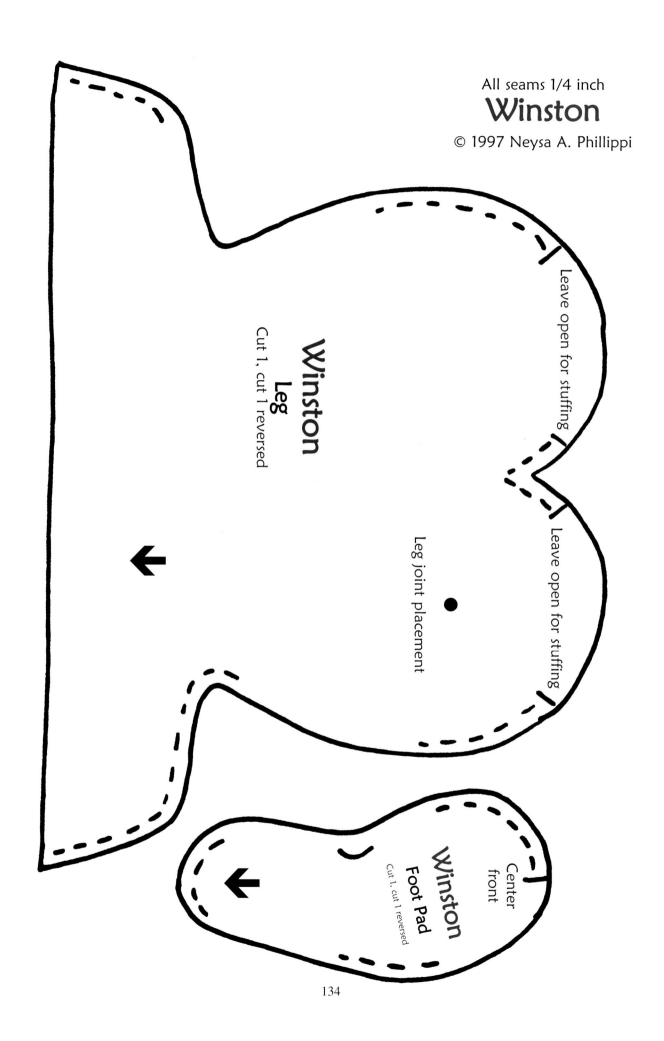

All seams 1/4 inch

Winston

© 1997 Neysa A. Phillippi

Leave open for stuffing

Leave open for stuffing

Winston
Leg
Cut 1, cut 1 reversed

Leg joint placement

Winston
Foot Pad
Cut 1, cut 1 reversed

Center front

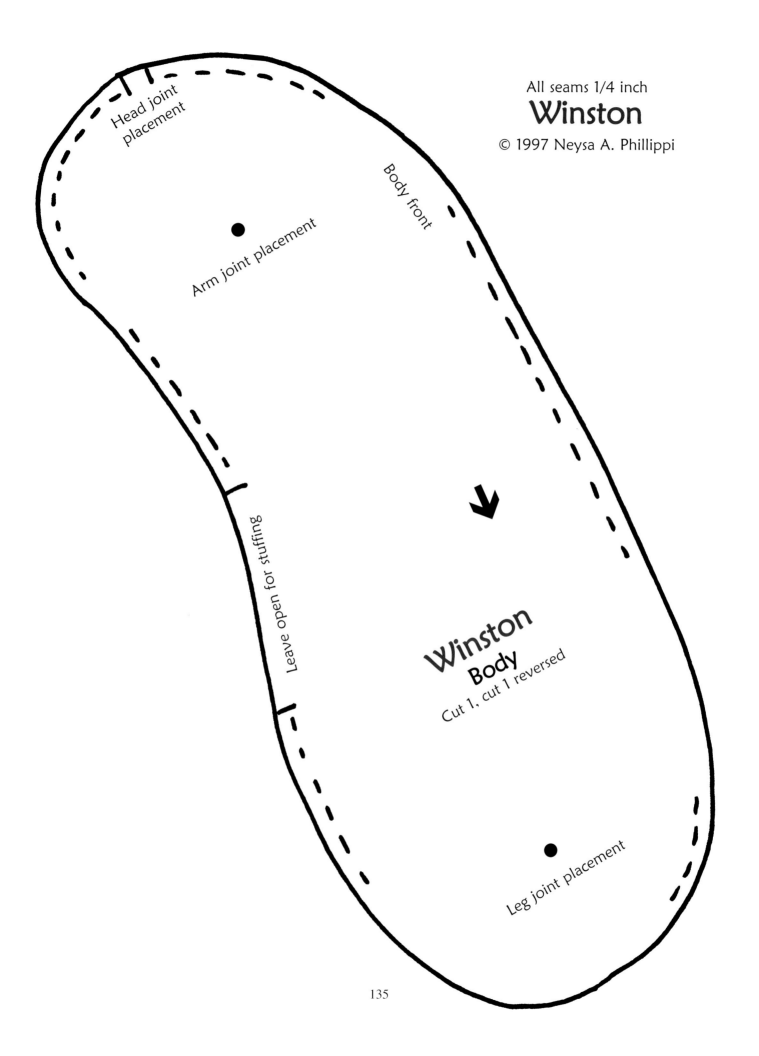

All seams 1/4 inch
Winston
© 1997 Neysa A. Phillippi

Head joint placement

Arm joint placement

Body front

Leave open for stuffing

Winston
Body
Cut 1, cut 1 reversed

Leg joint placement

Winston

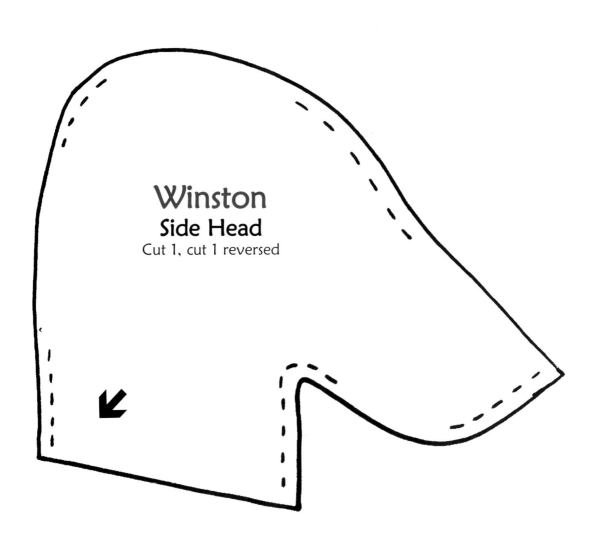

Winston
Side Head
Cut 1, cut 1 reversed

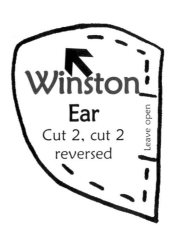

Winston
Ear
Cut 2, cut 2 reversed

Leave open

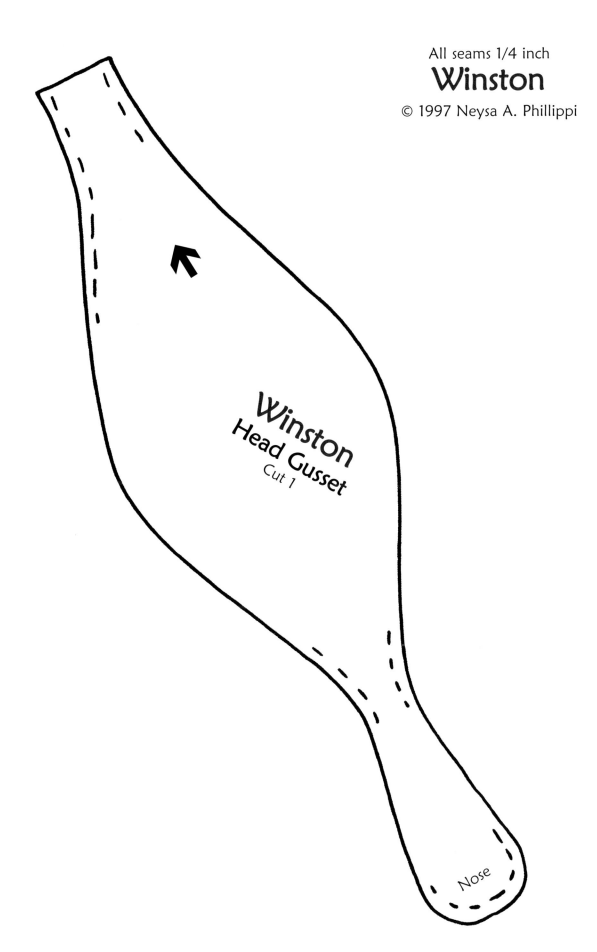

All seams 1/4 inch
Winston
© 1997 Neysa A. Phillippi

Winston
Head Gusset
Cut 1

Nose

137

All seams 1/4 inch
Winston
© 1997 Neysa A. Phillippi

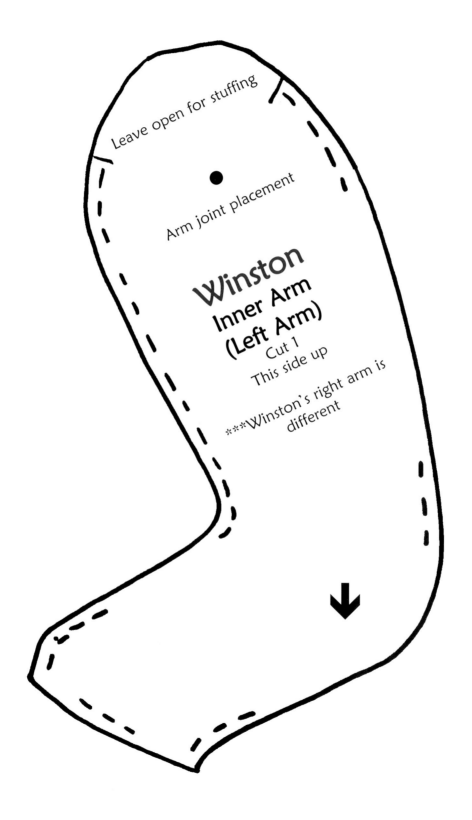

Leave open for stuffing

• Arm joint placement

Winston
Inner Arm
(Left Arm)
Cut 1
This side up

***Winston's right arm is different

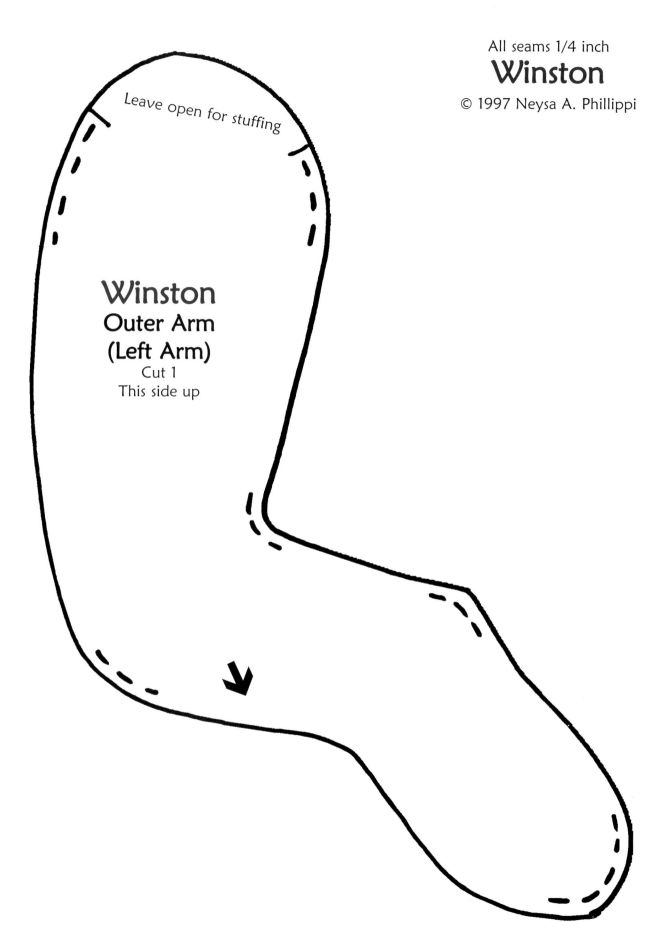

All seams 1/4 inch
Winston
© 1997 Neysa A. Phillippi

Leave open for stuffing

Winston
Outer Arm
(Left Arm)
Cut 1
This side up

139

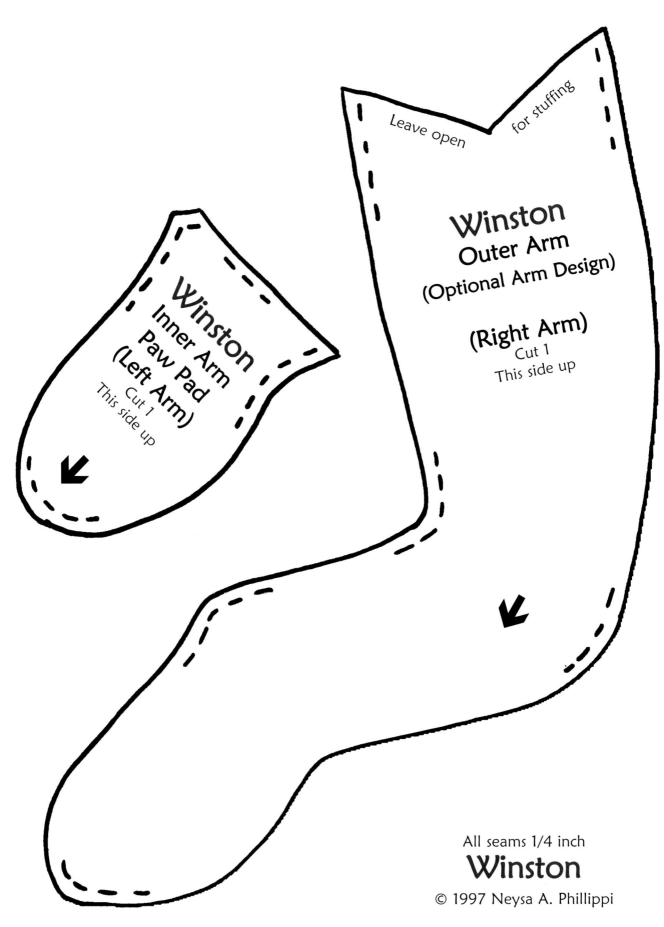

Winston
Inner Arm
Paw Pad
(Left Arm)
Cut 1
This side up

Leave open for stuffing

Winston
Outer Arm
(Optional Arm Design)

(Right Arm)
Cut 1
This side up

All seams 1/4 inch
Winston
© 1997 Neysa A. Phillippi

All seams 1/4 inch

Winston

© 1997 Neysa A. Phillippi

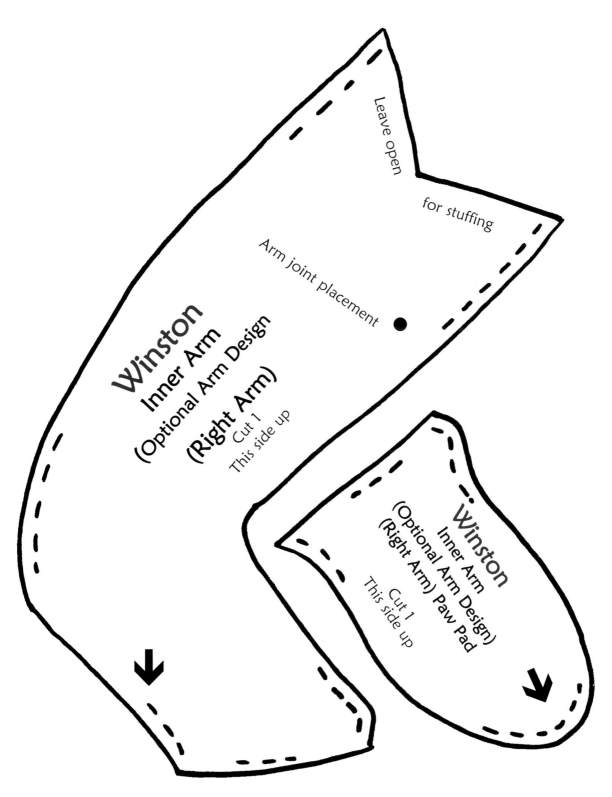

Leave open

for stuffing

Arm joint placement

Winston
Inner Arm
(Optional Arm Design)
(Right Arm)
Cut 1
This side up

Winston
Inner Arm
(Optional Arm Design)
(Right Arm) Paw Pad
Cut 1
This side up

Artists' Secrets for Making Better Bears

This tip works for all sizes of bears. To round out muzzles and the top of heads: On existing and new patterns – mark the matching points on the gusset and side head pieces where the eyes will be inserted or where the gusset widens. When assembling, slide the marked point of the side-head piece SLIGHTLY FORWARD of the marked point on the gusset. By easing in the little bit of extra length on the outside of the gusset and along the top of the head in the gusset, you will create a more rounded profile for stuffing."
Roberta Kasnick Ripperger, Creative Design Studio

After I sew my pattern pieces, and before turning them right side out, I put a thin line of the fray check at the point where the seam will be continued (when closing the seam). This way, you avoid fraying, but you also have a "stiff line" along which to sew your ladder stitch by … since it is stiff, then it folds at exactly the seam allowance that you have used for the machine stitching.

When teaching classes, I find it is much easier for the students to achieve even, consistent footpads, without puckers, by doing the following: I have the students put small "basting" stitches (by hand) around the footpads before sewing, either by hand or by machine. They are not standard "basting" stitches, but more like knots. I have the students fold the footpad in half, and mark it. Then I have them make a stitch on the center back footpad, then the front center, and then while "easing" the remaining pads, I put a stitch halfway between the front and back stitch, on each side...then another between those two, and so on. I use more stitches if the footpad is bigger. Then as you can imagine, it makes it easier to sew pads on without pins, and it is almost foolproof.
Kelli Frantik, Legacy Bears

Don't try to make everything absolutely perfect/balanced/proportioned when designing your bears. If you take a slide rule approach to bear design, you may end up with a perfectly proportioned, perfectly sewn ted… but what you miss is the "bearsonality." It is the little quirks and differences, just like with people, that make your bears stand out. Have FUN when you design and sew and everything else will fall into place.
Jutta Cyr, Bearaphanalia®

When putting in eyes, I use waxed dental floss instead of heavy thread. I found that I kept breaking the thread when I tried to pull it tight. Waxed dental floss doesn't break and the little bit of wax seems to keep the knots together.

I sew my paw pads by hand. However, ultrasuede is very difficult to pin, so I use small alligator clips to hold ultra-suede pads in place. This also works well for sewing any area that is curved and difficult to pin.
Linda Minter, Stellar Bears

Tools of the trade: 1) Sunbeam Steam Valet—a jet of steam directed to the fur that is either unruly or going the wrong direction, can bring style and change the appearance of your bear. After steaming and redirecting the fur with a finger tip brush, hold in place with scotch tape until the fur is dry. 2) Trimming shears—approximately 5 inches in size. Be sure to purchase top quality from a beauty supply house. Fur can be trimmed around the face, on top of the nose, etc. and won't have that chopped look of scissors."
Virginia Jasmer, Jazzbears

Three Stitch Ear: after threading your needle, attach the thread to the head gusset where you want the top of the ear to be positioned. Then run your needle through the top of your ear, run the thread back through the head gusset where you came out with your first stitch. Next run the needle out of the side head where the other end of the ear will be attached, attach the thread to the ear and run the needle back into the side head where your needle came out. Next pull your needle out in the middle of these two stitches but slightly more to the back of the head (to make a cupped ear). Run your needle through the center of the ear then back into the head where your needle came out. Pull the thread tightly and securely, and your ear is on.
Celia Baham, Celia's Teddies

To create the illusion of airbrushing, use Prisma oil pencils. You can create highlights and shadows by using light and dark colors. Remove excess pencil oil with a cosmetic sponge. Areas to work on: inside of the ear, outer ear, eye socket, around the nose and mouth, and cheek blush.
Robert Zacher, Robert Zacher Originals

If you want to make a different bear from what you see at shows, try dying your mohair. Start with a white or natural color and use liquid dyes, which are easier for measuring and getting the same color again. Dye wetted mohair in a tub, turning several times so you get an even color throughout the mohair. Try mixing colors in a measuring cup, coming up with a variety of colors not even on the market. Happy Coloring!
Terry Hayes, Pendleton's Teddy Bears

Two important considerations in making your bear patterns is the addition of notches on the pattern pieces and marking for the "Straight of the goods." These are essential in clothing design/construction in order to make the garment lie straight on the body and are equally important in laying out the bear pattern pieces on the mohair and subsequently pinning the pieces together for a perfect match – this of course is where the old-fashioned notches come in handy. If your pattern pieces are correctly placed and notches matched – the chances of getting a crooked body or limbs etc. are greatly reduced. I always make my pattern pieces on clear acetate, which I buy at an art supply store. This way I can mark the straight of the fabric on the pattern and then line it up with the warp thread in the fabric. The notches cut out easily in the acetate and trace easily onto the mohair because of the rigidity of the acetate.

Blanche Blakeny, Blakeny Bears

Trimming a bear's snout for a "clean" look – no bristles in the seams! After cutting out my pattern pieces, and before pinning and sewing, I shave my bear's snout and neck edges. Shaving can be done with an electric shaver or trimmed with scissors. I shave "bare" 1/2" to 1" (depending on the size of the bear) from the nose tip down to the mouth, and the gusset nose tip area the same as the nose to mouth. After I shave "bare" the nose areas, I like to work from the back of the snout to the front when I continue shaving. Starting at the back of the snout, I shave very slowly towards the front by tilting the shaver down, graduating the size of the mohair – longer mohair at the back of the snout to shorter mohair towards the front meeting the bare nose/mouth area which we already shaved bare previously. I trim with scissors a few hairs along the seam line and a small circle where the eyes will be attached. I then shave 1/2" to 1" depending on the size of the bear, the neck edge or bottom of the head and gusset pieces where the neck edge will be gathered around the joint without all the bulky mohair getting in the way.

Karen Meer, The Mad Hatted Bear

When working with real fur, you should always first check the pelts to make sure that there are no splits or that dry rotting has taken place. If the pelt is dry rotted, it will be very brittle and will easily fall apart. Once you have determined that it is workable, a lining such as muslin or even the lining that was in the garment to begin with will work. Cut your pattern out of the lining and then out of the fur. Baste your lining to your fur then stitch your pieces together as normal. I don't recommend using a fusible lining because the number one rule with real fur is do not place in, near, or around heat. Ironing in a fusible lining could create dry rot down the road. If you omit the task of lining your real fur bear, you will end up with seams that will pop or pieces that will not turn right side out.

Dina Denning, Creative Stitches by Dina, Inc.

When stitching the nose, use watered-down tacky glue. Add a small amount with a paintbrush to the nose area when you are stitching the nose. This will hold the yarn in place and the bear's nose will never separate. Tacky glue will wash out and it dries clear. Use sparingly – too much and it will seep through the yarn and make a hard spot.

If you have one joint that you can't get as tight as the rest, try a rubber band between the body and the uncooperative arm or leg. Do this after the bear is finished.

For a more professional finish pull your knots to the inside for a smoother finish when closing your seams or stitching on ears.

Don't have an airbrush? Try oil pastels. Be sure to wipe the excess off with a clean cloth. See the photograph of Winston. Water-based tole paint will work also.

Find soft sculpting time-consuming? Incorporate more drastic shapes into your designs, for example on your side head and gusset to draw the eyes in closer together.

Hate trimming your bear's muzzles with scissors? Buy a beard and mustache trimmer such as the Norelco Maverick T-3000. It has a smaller trimmer attached that works for small areas and a larger trimmer for the tops of the muzzle. The T-3000 is also battery/electrically operated. Your local beauty supply house should carry a small trimmer that will work just as well. Need something for large areas? Try dog grooming trimmers; I use these to trim rat tails and legs.

There is no right or wrong way to make a bear. Never be afraid to ask how or why!

Neysa A. Phillippi, *Purely Neysa*

Invaluable Sources
for books, supplies, patterns, fabrics and tours

Supplies

Intercal Trading Group
1760 Monrovia Avenue,
Suite A-17
Costa Mesa, CA 92627
Telephone: 949-645-9396
Fax: 949-645-5471
www.intercaltg.com
fur, eyes, etc.

Bear Street – Dale Junker
415 W. Foothill Boulevard
Claremont, CA 91711
Telephone: 909-625-2995
fur, eyes, joints, patterns, kits

Edinburgh Imports, Inc.
POB 340
Newbury Park, CA 91319-0340
Telephone: 805-376-1700
Fax: 805-376-1711
WWW.EDINBURGH.COM
fur, eyes, etc

L.Z. Products
Attention: Ivy Tuber, tell her
Neysa sent you!
2121 W. 21st Street
Chicago, IL 60608
Telephone: 773-847-0572
Fax: 773-847-1171
*ultra suede, velour upholstery
fabric*

Bolek's Craft Supplies
P.O. Box 465
330 N. Tuscarawas Avenue
Dover, OH 44622-0465
Telephone: 330-364-8878
plastic joints

Golden Fun Kits
P.O. Box 10697
Edgemont Branch
Golden, CO 80401-0600
Mail order only
eyes, music boxes, patterns

Reinhold Lesch GmbH
Oeslauer StraBe 121-123
D-96472 Rodental
Germany
Telephone: 011-49-95 63 72 21 0
Fax: 011-49-95 63 72 21 22
www.Lesch.de
*eyes, growlers, doll wigs,-
tell them Neysa sent you!*

Enterprise Art
2860 Roosevelt Blvd.
Clearwater, FL 34620
craft supplies

Purely Neysa
45 Gorman Avenue
Indiana, PA 15701-2244
Telephone: 724-349-1225
Fax: 724-349-3903
Email: purelyneysa@yourinter.net
woven plush from Belgium

Name Maker, Inc.
PO Box 43821
Atlanta, GA 30378-3601
Telephone: 800-241-2890
Fax: 404-691-7711
fabric name tags

Monterey Mills
PO Box 271
Janesville, WI 53547
Telephone: 608-754-2866
Fax: 608-754-3750
*Fake fur, stuffing —- Quality A,
costs about $1.85 a pound in 20
pound bags, feeds out in a coil,
minimum order: $100)*

Newark dressmaker supply.
6473 Ruch Road
PO Box 20730
Lehigh Valley, PA 18002-0730
Telephone: 800-736-6783
thread, needles, etc.

Dollspart™ Supply Company, Inc.
The Teddy Works™
8000 Cooper Avenue, Bldg. 28
Glendale, NY 11385
Telephone: 800-336-DOLL
Fax: 718-326-4971

Tandy Leather & Craft
Call for a catalog
800-555-3130

The Leather Factory
2435 W. Pawnee
PO Box 13100
Wichita, KS 67213
Telephone: 559-942-7773
800-984-7147
leather, rivets, etc

North State Supply Co, Inc.
390 Fergesen Road
Homer City, PA 15748
Telephone: 724-479-3511
*cotter pins, bolts, nuts
pop rivets and pop rivet guns in
volume for great prices*

Artemis
179 High Street
South Portland, ME 04106
Telephone: 888-233-5187
Fax: 207-741-2497
Email: artemis@ime.net
*hand-dyed, bias cut Hannah silk
& satin ribbons*

Sandy's Victorian Trims
7417 North Knoxville Avenue
Peoria, IL 61614
Telephone: 309-689-1943
Fax: 309-689-1942
silk ribbon

Standard Doll Co.
23-83 31st Street
L.I.C., NY 11105
Telephone: 800-543-6557
Fax: 718-274-4231

Patterns

Purely Neysa
Patterns of Bears Gone "Buy"
Neysa A. Phillippi
45 Gorman Avenue
Indiana, PA 15701-2244
Telephone: 724-349-1225
Fax: 724-349-3903
Email: purelyneysa@yourinter.net
*creatures, patterns and woven
plush*

Celia's Teddies
Celia Baham
1562 San Joaquin Avenue
San Jose, CA 95118
Telephone: 408-266-8129
Fax: 408-978-2888
Email: Celiasteds@aol.com
www.Celiasteddies.com
bears, cats and patterns

Robert Zacher Originals
Robert Zacher
416 E. Broadway
Waukesha, WI 53186
Telephone: 262-544-4739
Fax: 262-544-6676
*Limited editions, bear and
animal patterns*

Creative Design
Roberta Kasnick Ripperger
P.O. Box 1381
Elmhurst, IL 60126
Telephone: 630-834-2073
Fax: 630-834-1104
Www. Beyond-basic-bears.com
Email: rkr4cds@mediaone.com
*miniature bears, patterns and
fabrics*

For pattern catalogs contact
each artist for prices and
payment methods.

Teddy Bear Tours

Off the Wall Creative Tours
featuring the "Artists for Artists"
Annual European Tours
Neysa A. Phillippi
45 Gorman Avenue
Indiana, PA 15701-2244
Tel 724 349-1225
Fax 724 349-3903
Email: offthewalltours@yourinter.net

Books

**The Ultimate Handbook for
Making Teddy Bears**
By Linda Mullins
Hobby House Press, Inc., 1998

**Teddy Bear Art:
How to Design and Make Great
Teddy Bears**
by Jennifer Laing
Hobby House Press, Inc., 1998

**The Complete Book
of Teddy-Bear Making
Techniques**
by Alicia Merrett & Ann Stephens
Running Press Book Publishers,
1998

**The Teddy Bear Sourcebook
for Collectors and Artists**
by Betterway Books
Betterway Books, 1995

**Teddy Bears Past & Present
A Collector's Identification Guide**
by Linda Mullins
Hobby House Press, Inc., 1986

The Ultimate Teddy Bear Book
by Pauline Cockrill
Dorling Kindersley, Inc., 1991

Books about "real" bears

Polar Bear
By Dan Guravich
& Downs Matthews
Chronicle Books, 1993

**Bears: Majestic Creatures
of the Wild**
Consulting Editor:
Ian Stirling, Ph.D
Canadian Wildlife Service
Rodale Press, Inc., 1993

Bears: Their Life and Behavior
By Art Wolfe
& William Ashworth
Crown Publishers, Inc., 1992